MW00395646

STRENGTH FROM WEAKNESS: GROWING THROUGH SUFFERING

By Harriet Hill

Contributors: Margaret Hill, Godfrey Loum, Uwingeneye Baraka Paulette, Charles Adu Twumasi, Desiree Guyton, Carol King

Trauma Healing Institute
traumahealinginstitute.org
101 North Independence Mall East
Philadelphia PA 19106
Email: support@traumahealinginstitute.org

Reviewers: Richard Winter, Richard Baggé, Philip Monroe, Debbie Wolcott, Peter Edman, Heather Drew
Editor: Heather Drew
Illustrations: Ian Dale
Design: Caleb W. Cliff
Typesetting: Caleb W. Cliff

For training in how to use this book to carry out trauma healing ministry, visit TraumaHealingInstitute.org or write to info@traumahealinginstitute.org.

ISBN 978-1-58516-331-1 / ABS Item 125178 (Paperback)

Printed in the United States of America

They will be like trees that the LORD himself has planted.
They will all do what is right, and God will be praised for what he has done.
They will rebuild cities that have long been in ruins.

Isaiah 61:3–4

When I am weak, then I am strong.

2 Corinthians 12:9–10

Table of contents

Introduction

This book is the second in a series, intended to be used after the first book, *Healing the Wounds of Trauma: How the Church Can Help*. The first book helps people heal from trauma and loss using biblical and mental health principles.

This second book, *Strength from Weakness*, helps people grow through their suffering and become more resilient so they are better prepared to face suffering in the future. It helps them explore more layers of their trauma and pain, and experience deeper layers of healing. It helps them gain skills to connect with others in healthier ways so that the underlying causes of trauma are addressed, and a strong, vibrant community is (re-)established. Finally, it helps people find and fulfill their purpose in life. This may include advocating for justice for those who are suffering from oppression. All these things work together to increase resilience.

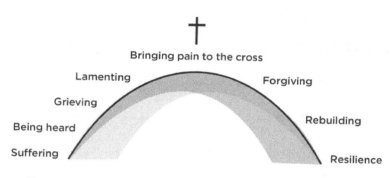

Figure 1. Healing the Wounds of Trauma and Strength from Weakness work together to increase resilience.

Figure 1 shows the emphasis of the two books: *Healing the Wounds of Trauma* gives more attention to the first half of the trauma healing arc, while Strength from Weakness gives more attention to the second half.

Both books are most effective when used in groups led by trained facilitators. Contact info@traumahealinginstitute.org to find a facilitator or a session for training facilitators.

For guidance in leading groups please refer to *Healing the Wounds of Trauma: Facilitator Guide for Healing Groups*. Leaders should use the principles learned there as they lead these lessons.

Each of the lessons will take a minimum of 1.5 hours. If time allows, do all of the lessons. If your time is limited, select the ones that are most relevant to your group. Suggested amounts of time are given for each section to give you an idea of how to plan your time. Use the time you need to engage the topic. Instructions for the facilitator are included in italics to guide you through the lessons. Read at least some of suggested Scripture passages together, as God's Word is important in the healing process. Some key quotes appear in boxes throughout the lesson; decide when or whether to read them in the group.

This book is to be used by a certified trauma healing facilitator. To be trained in using this book, go to traumahealinginstitute.org/events. Answers to frequently asked questions about how to use this material can be found on the THI facilitator website.

This product is not intended to diagnose, treat, or cure any disease. It does not take the place of professional counseling. If you use this product, you show that you understand this.

Onion devotional

Before you begin:

- You will need one onion per participant. It is good to refrigerate the onions for 24 hours to lessen the odor.
- If possible, do this exercise outdoors.
- Place 1 lighted candle on each table to absorb the odor. Also, it can be helpful to open windows and doors for fresh air.

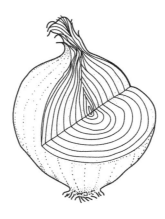

Figure 2. Trauma has layers like an onion

In this devotional we will:

- Discover layers with occur in trauma and healing.
- Consider how to be more patient with the process of healing.

Exercise:

Strength from Weakness helps us look at deeper layers of pain that we may still be carrying.

What can we learn from the onion about layers of trauma and healing?

Get quiet inside and begin peeling layers off your onion. Use only your hands.

What do you observe? What do you feel? Smell? Just observe; don't think about how this applies to healing.

When everyone has finished, share what you observed in the large group. Then reflect on implications for layers of trauma and healing asking open ended questions. For example, when you first realize you are traumatized, you may be angry, then as time goes on, you may be sad, and later you may be anxious. Discuss this as a group.

Lesson 1. Wrestling with God

Before you begin:

- For Section 1: Decide how you will present the story.
  - Prepare slips of paper with Bible verses.
  - Prepare a flip chart diagram of 3 villages.
- For Section 2: Prepare a flip chart picture of an ATM machine.
- For Section 3: Prepare slips of paper with Bible verses.

In this lesson we will:

- Discover how to make better sense of our experiences of suffering and faith.
- Learn that grieving may involve wrestling with God.
- See that wrestling with God can be an evidence of our faith rather than doubt.
- Practice letting go of trying to control God.
- Experience a time of resting in God's love.

Lesson introduction

Have you ever had a time when you could not make sense of what happened to you, given your beliefs in God's care and protection? This is often our experience after trauma and loss. Like Jacob wrestled with the angel in Genesis 32:22-32, we may wrestle with God as we try to understand what has happened to us. It can be part of fighting the good fight of faith (1 Timothy 6:12). We may lament, struggle, and argue! Many people in the Bible wrestled with God. In this lesson, we will look at Job.

1. Job wrestles with God (30 min)

For groups already familiar with the story, go directly to the large group discussion question.
There was a man whose name was Job. He was the richest man in his region with many farms and animals. He had a big family. He was a good man who respected God and refused to do evil.

One day Satan was with God, and God asked him if he had noticed how faithful and good Job had been. Satan replied, "Why shouldn't he respect you? You make him successful in whatever he does. Take away everything he owns, and he will curse you to your face." God told Satan, "All right, do what you want with anything that belongs to him, but don't harm Job."

Soon after that, a messenger came to Job and said, "Enemies have attacked and stolen your oxen and donkeys and have killed your servants." While he was still speaking, a second messenger said, "God sent down a fire that killed your sheep and your servants." While he was still speaking, a third messenger came and said, "Enemies stole your camels and killed your servants." While he was still speaking, a fourth messenger came and said, "Your children were having a party and a storm came and blew the house down, crushing all of your children."

After hearing all this, Job tore his clothes and shaved his head because of his great sorrow. He knelt on the ground, worshiped God and said, "We bring nothing at birth; we take nothing with us at death. The Lord alone gives and takes. Praise the name of the LORD!" In spite of everything, Job did not sin or accuse God of doing wrong.

A little while later, God asked Satan what he thought of Job now. Satan said, "Strike Job's own body with pain, and he will curse you to your face." So the LORD replied, "All right! Make Job suffer as much as you want, but just don't kill him."

Then Satan made sores break out all over Job's body. Job sat by the garbage dump and scraped his sores with a piece of broken pottery. His wife said to him, "Why don't you curse God and die?" Job answered, "Don't talk like a fool! If we accept blessings from God, we must accept trouble as well." In all that happened, Job never once said anything against God.

Soon after, three of his friends came to comfort him. When they saw how much he suffered, they cried and wailed. Then they sat with him in silence for seven days .

Finally, Job broke the silence and cursed the day he was born. Then his friends told him that his suffering was because of his sins and the sins of his children. Job insisted he had not sinned, but they were sure that if he were innocent, God would not have let these things happen. They accused him over and over to try to get him to confess. Finally, Job says, "You are terrible comforters!" Rather than comforting Job, they increased his pain.

Finally, Job asked God to explain what was happening. God responded by asking him, "How did I lay the earth's foundation? Were you there? Can you order the clouds to send a downpour, or will lightning flash at your command? Did you give horses their strength?" On and on, God asked Job question after question that showed he was more powerful and wiser than Job. Finally Job answered, "I have talked about things that are beyond my understanding."

God was angry with Job's friends because they said things about God that were not true. God told them to bring a sacrifice and Job would pray for them so that they would be forgiven. After this, God blessed Job with ten new children and twice as much land and animals as he had before. He lived to an old age and saw his great-grand-children.

LARGE GROUP DISCUSSION

What happened to Job?

Share feedback in the large group and then add anything from below that has not already been mentioned:

- He was a wealthy man with many children.
- Tragedy struck and he lost everything in a day.
- His body was covered with sores.
- He was a good man who feared God.
- His friends came to comfort him but actually made his suffering worse.

Job and his friends believed that God was just, and life was predictable:

If we obey God, he blesses us.
If we sin, God brings us suffering.

These beliefs made them feel like they could control God: if they obeyed God, he had to bless them. Their lives were proof that this was true: they had obeyed God and they were wealthy and healthy.

When Job lost everything, his friends concluded that he must have sinned. The book of Job tells us something they did not know--that Job had not sinned (*Job 1:1, 8, 22*). For Job, nothing made sense anymore. His undeserved suffering challenged what he understood about God.

SMALL GROUP DISCUSSION

1. In Job 7, what feelings did Job express as he wrestled with God? What word pictures did he use?[1]
2. How did God respond?
   a. *Job 38:1–5*
   b. *Job 39:9–12*
   c. *Job 40:3–10*
3. How did Job respond in the end? *Job 42:1–6*
4. Who was God angry with? Why was God angry with them? *Job 42:7–8*

---

[1] Job is well worth studying in more depth. For example, explore chapter 6:1-17, 28-30; chapter 9:11-35; chapter 10: 1-22; or chapter 21:1-17.

Share feedback in the large group and then add anything from below that has not already been mentioned:

- God made the universe and there is order in it (*Job 6*), but there are also wild things. We can no more control God than we can control the wild donkeys (*Job 39:9-12*).
- Job surrenders to God's loving control as the creator and sustainer of the universe. He sees the foolishness of thinking he could understand or control God (*Job 42:1-6*).
- God never condemns Job for asking hard, angry questions. Instead, God is angry with Job's friends for thinking they knew why Job suffered. He makes them offer a sacrifice and, rather than being bitter towards them, Job prays for them (*Job 42:7-8*).

LARGE GROUP DISCUSSION

Which of these points mean the most to you and why?

In the *Healing the Wounds of Trauma* lesson on Grieving, we learned about how to grieve our losses by going on a "grief journey" through three villages: the Village of Anger and Denial, the Village of No Hope, and the Village of New Beginnings. Job takes this painful journey.

Village 1: In Job 1–2, he seems untouched by these tragedies. He says, "Naked I came from my mother's womb and naked I will depart" (1:21). He refuses to complain (2:10) and praises God.

Village 2: In Job 3–41, his tone changes. He wrestles with God to try to make sense of what happened.

Village 3: In Job 42, he says, "Now my eyes have seen you!"

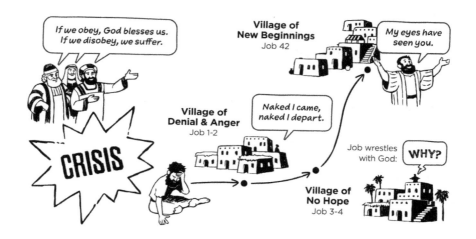

LARGE GROUP DISCUSSION

Think of a time you went through suffering.

1. Did anyone insist that it was because you had sinned? If yes, how did it feel?
2. When you were suffering, did you learn anything new about God? Explain.

2. We do not control God (10 min)

Do a skit of a person getting money from an ATM[2]:

- Jane puts a credit/debit card into the ATM.
- She specifies the amount.
- She withdraws the cash and possibly a receipt.
- She has a big smile.

Figure 4. God is not like an ATM machine

[2]If ATMs are not known in your area, use the example of a shop. You pay the right amount of money to the shop keeper and he or she hands you the item.

1. Can you think of times when you or others have expected God to respond like an ATM machine?" If yes, explain the thinking behind it.
2. How is our relationship with God different from our relationship with an ATM machine?

Share feedback in the large group and then add anything from below that has not already been mentioned:

- We may share the same beliefs that Job and his friends had (example: if we obey God, he has to bless us just like using an ATM machine). But our relationship with God is one of love, and love requires freedom.
- We have freedom to obey or disobey, and God has freedom to respond, too.
- At times, our emotions may become heated.
- We may feel angry at God by the way he surprises us, not doing our bidding.
- We may not understand or see God's love.

---

3. What does the Bible teach about suffering? (25 min)

What do these passages tell us about suffering and sin?

> Hebrews 11:32–40
> Luke 6:20–26
> Romans 8:18–23
> Matthew 5:45b
> John 10:10
> Hebrews 12:5–11
> 1 Peter 3:17

Share feedback in the large group and then add anything from below that has not already been mentioned:

- Many people of great faith suffered; they are referred to as those "of whom the world was not worthy" (*Hebrews 11:32-40*).
- Jesus said that those who are poor, hungry, weeping, hated, mocked, or excluded are blessed, but suffering awaits those who are rich, fat, and happy (*Luke 6:20-26*).
- We live in a fallen world where all creation is groaning, we are groaning, and the Holy Spirit is groaning (*Romans 8:18-23*).
- Both good and bad people suffer (*Matthew 5:45b*).
- Satan continues to try to steal, kill, and destroy (*John 10:10*).
- Sometimes suffering means God is disciplining us in love so we improve (*Hebrews 12:5-11*).
- Sometimes we may suffer when we are doing good (*1 Peter 3:17*). We cannot conclude that suffering always means that we have sinned. God may be using our experience in ways we are not aware of.

---

4. What does faith look like in times of suffering? (15 min)

When we are suffering, what does faith look like? Sometimes it is a time to express our feelings of betrayal and disappointment openly to God in a lament, as we learned in *Healing the Wounds of Trauma*. The raw agony Job expressed provides us with a good example to follow.

SMALL GROUP DISCUSSION

1. Do you see wrestling with God as a sign of great faith or doubt? Explain your response.
2. Why do you think some people avoid wrestling with God? How do they avoid it?

Share feedback in the large group and then add anything from below that has not already been mentioned:

- God welcomes our hard questions.
- Our questions show that we believe God is there, that he is listening, that he cares, and that he will answer.
- When we wrestle with God about these hard questions, we often dislodge wrong beliefs.

- We grow through our suffering to a new level of knowing God—that he is in control, not us.
- This may seem scary, but in fact, it is a much more secure and correct understanding of life.
- Often, all we can know for sure is that God loves us.
- We will not always understand why certain things happen.

5. Closing exercise (10 min)

In many lament psalms, the psalmist wrestles with God like Job did. After wrestling and lamenting, the psalmist in Psalm 131 arrives at much the same place Job did: a place of peace and contentment. He compares himself to a weaned child.

SMALL GROUP DISCUSSION

While being weaned, how does a child act?
After being weaned, how does a child act?

DISCUSSION IN TWOS

1. Are you wrestling with God about anything? Explain.
2. Do you see any progress of being more at rest, like a weaned child? Explain.

Figure 5. Like a weaned child with its mother

INDIVIDUAL REFLECTION

Get quiet inside, close your eyes and listen to this psalm. Even if you are not completely at peace yet, imagine yourself for a moment as content as a weaned child.

> *My heart is not proud, Lord,*
> *my eyes are not haughty;*
> *I do not concern myself with great matters*
> *or things too wonderful for me.*
> *But I have calmed and quieted myself,*
> *I am like a weaned child with its mother;*
> *like a weaned child I am content. (Psalm 131:1–2 NIV)*

Before you begin:

- For Section 1 prepare slips of papers with group assignments.
- For Section 2 prepare slips of papers with Bible verses.
  - Prepare flip chart paper with 2 columns, one for good and one for evil.
  - Have paper and markers/colors/ pencil available for each person at their tables to participate in word art.
- For Section 3 make 4 copies of the skit and choose 4 people to act out the skit.
- For Section 3 prepare slips of paper with Bible verses.
- For Section 4 prepare slips of paper with Bible verses.
- Prepare flip chart paper with 2 columns, one for "Feeding good" and one for "Feeding evil."

In this lesson we will:

- Discuss the nature of good and evil.
- Explore ways to choose good in our lives.
- Identify areas where we are vulnerable to evil.
- Explore the principle of sowing and reaping.

Lesson introduction

Sometimes when we suffer, we see how evil people can be toward one another. How do people become so evil? And how can we choose to commit our lives to doing good?

If we are victims of trauma, the hurt we experienced can be an opportunity for Satan and evil to enter our lives (*Ephesians 4:27*). We may find ourselves hurting others in the same way we were hurt, even though we never intended to do this (*Romans 7:15*). Hurt people hurt people. We need to know where we are weak so we can be especially careful.

1. Cain and Abel (25 min)

After Adam and Eve were chased out of the Garden of Eden, Eve gave birth to two sons. The older son was called Cain, the younger Abel. When they grew up, Abel became a shepherd, and Cain became a farmer. After some time, Cain brought some of his harvest and gave it as an offering to the Lord. Then Abel brought the first lamb born of one of his sheep, killed it, and gave the best parts of it as an offering. The Lord was pleased with Abel and his offering, but he rejected Cain and his offering.[3]

Cain became furious and scowled in anger. Then the Lord said to Cain, "Why are you angry? Why that scowl on your face? If you had done the right thing, you would be smiling; but because you have done evil, sin is crouching at your door. It wants to rule you, but you must overcome it."

Then Cain said to Abel, "Let's go out in the fields." When they were out in the fields, Cain turned on his brother and killed him.

The Lord asked Cain, "Where is your brother Abel?"

He answered, "I don't know. Am I supposed to take care of my brother?"

Then the Lord said, "Why have you done this terrible thing? Your brother's blood is crying out to me from the ground, like a voice calling for revenge. You are placed under a curse and can no longer farm the soil. If you try to grow crops, the soil will not produce anything; you will be a homeless wanderer on the earth."

Cain pleaded with the Lord for mercy. He was afraid people would try to kill him. So God put a mark on him to warn anyone who met him not to kill him, and then God sent him away.

Much later in the New Testament, Abel is remembered as one who, by faith, offered a better offering than Cain (*Hebrews 11:4*). Cain is remembered as one who murdered his brother because his actions were evil, and his brother's were good (*1 John 3:12*).

(Genesis 4:1–16, adapted)

---

[3]Notice that the story says that Abel offered the best parts of the first lamb of one of his sheep, while it says Cain just brought some of his harvest.

Cain had choices in this story. Each time he made a wrong choice, he allowed evil to rule in his heart, which made it more difficult to do right. Have two groups use their imaginations to prepare the skits below. Other groups can reflect on the Bible story itself.

Group 1: Make a skit on how the story might have ended if Cain had not let sin rule over him when God rejected his offering.

Group 2: Make a skit of Cain telling the truth to God about where Abel was after he had killed him.

Other groups: Read the Bible story and discuss Cain's choices.

- In what ways did Cain's choices affect him?
- How did they affect those around him?
- How did Cain's choices affect his relationship with God?
- How could he have acted differently?

As you present the skits, discuss:

1. What do we learn from this story about how evil can grow in our hearts?
2. What makes it more difficult to choose to do what is right after having made a bad choice?
3. If you have ever felt like Cain, raise your hand.

---

2. The nature of good and evil (25 min)

What do these verses tell us about who is affected by evil and how they are affected?

> *Romans 3:23; 5:12*
> *Psalm 14:1–3*
> *1 Peter 5:8-9*
> *1 John 2:16*

Share feedback and then add anything from below that has not already been mentioned:

- All of us have sinned.
- All of us have the ability to do good and evil.
- We all need to beware of the pull inside us to do what we know is wrong. It is a daily challenge to choose good.

INDIVIDUAL REFLECTION

Write down the first three things that come to your mind when you think of what your culture considers to be:

A very good thing.

A very evil thing.

In the large group, have people share their ideas and create a list of everyone's answers [what the culture says is good and another list of what the culture says is evil].

Cultures define good and evil differently. For example, in some cultures being generous is better than anything else, while in others being on time is the mark of a good person. Although cultures vary, the Bible helps us understand the nature of good and evil for all people and cultures.

What do these passages tell us about the nature of good and evil?

> *John 8:44*
> *James 1:14-15*
> *Romans 6:16*
> *James 1:17-18*
> *Proverbs 19:23*
> *John 1:4-5*

Share feedback and then add anything from below that has not already been mentioned:

Good:
is pure and true (James 1:17-18)
leads to life, wisdom, and feeling content (Proverbs 19:23).
is stronger than evil and will never be extinguished (John 1:4-5).

Evil:
is based in lies and deceit (John 8:44). Like Satan in the Garden of Eden, or with Jesus in the desert, evil mixes truth with lies to trick us.
promises to make us happy, but it cannot deliver or satisfy; it only leaves us longing for more (James 1:14-15).
leads to folly and destruction (Romans 6:16).

Art Exercise

Think about the nature of good and evil. Divide a paper in half and do a drawing (or word art) of evil on one half and good on the other. Come back together so a few can share what they made with the large group.

---

3. Know your enemy (15 min)

Act out this skit:

Characters:

John
Tempter
The Holy Spirit

John sits in a chair with the *Tempter* whispering from behind his left ear, and *the Holy Spirit* from behind his right ear.

John is the treasurer of his church. He has the cashbox in his house. He has just heard that his mother is very ill and needs money to go to the hospital. It is the end of the month and he has no money of his own left.

Tempter: Just take some of the church's money. You can always put it back next month.

The Holy Spirit: No, don't steal!

Tempter: Don't you care about your mother? She needs your help!

The Holy Spirit: Think of other ways of getting some money. Maybe a friend would help?

Tempter: Why should you bother your friends? The money is right there in front of you!

The Holy Spirit: The church has trusted you to look after their money; don't break their trust.

Tempter: No one needs to know that you have taken the money. Just do it!

The Holy Spirit: The Bible says, "You shall not steal." Only bad things come from breaking God's law.

Tempter: But God will understand in this case. After all, it is your mother's life!

The Holy Spirit: But think! Is there a friend you ask to lend you money until you get your salary?

Tempter: No! How shameful to ask for help!

SMALL GROUP DISCUSSION

What should John do?

LARGE GROUP DISCUSSION

Read all or some of these passages and discuss:

How did these people in the Bible let themselves be deceived by evil? What can we learn from their mistakes?

> *Adam and Eve: Genesis 3:1–4*
> *David with Bathsheba: 2 Samuel 11:1–5*
> *Achan: Joshua 7:20–21*
> *Ananias and Sapphira: Acts 5:1–11*
> *Saul and Samuel: 1 Samuel 13:7b-14*

Share feedback in the large group and add anything from below not already mentioned:

- Evil cannot take any ground we don't give it. In all of these Bible stories, people had a choice, and we do, too (*Matthew 7:13-14; 23:37b*). We need to be familiar with Satan's evil schemes to not be outwitted by him (*2 Corinthians 2:11*).
- Our hearts are deceitful and corrupt (*Jeremiah 17:9*). We can rationalize our sins by telling ourselves it is not really wrong, not wrong for us, or not wrong "under these circumstances." Or we may be good most of the time but have a secret sin. We need to keep a close watch over our deceitful hearts.
- We need discernment because evil is always mixed with at least some good.
- Shame may keep us from telling ourselves and others the truth.

Even with our best efforts, we will make mistakes (*Romans 7:14-15*). When that happens, we can confess our short comings to God and be assured of his forgiveness (*1 John 1:9*). To resist temptations that wrong going forward, we need to remember that God promises to help us when we are tempted and to show us a way out (*1 Corinthians 10:13*).

---

4. The principle of sowing and reaping (20 min)

The Bible tells us that we will reap what we sow (*Galatians 6:7-8*). This does not mean that we will always reap exactly and only what we sow, or that we will reap immediately, or that we will always sow good things. But generally over time, we reap what we sow, as illustrated in this story:

> A grandfather was talking to his grandson. Times were very difficult. The people were poor and starving. People were frustrated and there was great unrest.
>
> The grandfather said, "I feel as if I have two wolves fighting in my heart. One wolf is vengeful, angry, violent. The other wolf is loving and compassionate."
>
> The grandson asked him, "Which wolf will win the fight in your heart?"
>
> The grandfather replied, "The one I feed."

Figure 6. What you feed wins

LARGE GROUP DISCUSSION

We sow good to show our love for God in response to his love for us (*1 John 4:19; John 15:10; Ephesians 2:8-10*), not to try to earn his love or blessings.

1. In what ways do people feed good in their lives?
2. In what ways do people feed evil in their lives?
3. How do these Bible passages underscore this story about the wolves (*James 1:14-15*)?
4. So how can we nourish good in our lives?

- We can sow something small (the wind) and reap something big (a whirlwind) (Hosea 8:7a).
- If we feed evil, it leads to a foretaste of hell on earth. If we feed good, it leads to a foretaste of heaven on earth (Ephesians 1:13-14).

SMALL GROUP DISCUSSION

Read the verses below. What do they say about feeding good and evil in our lives?

Ephesians 5:11
John 3:19–21
John 8:32
Hebrews 10:24–25; 1 Corinthians 15:33
John 8:44; 10:10
Philippians 2: 3–4

Share feedback in the large group and then add anything from below that has not already been mentioned:

Feeding good in your life	Feeding evil in your life
Light: Seeking the light. Exposing secrets.	Darkness: Keeping secrets
Truth: Feeding on the truth.	Lies: Feeding on lies.
Patience: Wait for the right thing in the right way.	Impatience: Willing to steal, kill, and destroy to accomplish goals.
Being humble and caring for others.	Being proud and self-absorbed. Selfish.
Fellowship with people who love good.	Keeping company with people who love evil.

5. Closing exercise (5 min)

INDIVIDUAL REFLECTION

1. What does the tempter whisper in your ear? In what ways are you are likely to be tempted to do evil?
2. How have you seen God's mercy when you have made bad choices?
3. If you have been deceived by evil, what practical steps can you take?

Pray for the group, that they will have the courage and strength to do what they should, to overcome evil in their lives and promote good.

Lesson 3. Generational trauma and blessing

Before you begin:

- For Section 2: Have a large piece of paper for each person available at the tables.
- For Section 6: Have a small stone and a marker for each person at the tables.

In this lesson we will:

- Explore ways that trauma and blessing can be passed through generations.
- Discuss the tension between being a victim of generational trauma and taking responsibility for our own choices.
- Identify generational trauma and blessing in our own families.
- Come up with ideas of how we can stop the cycle of generational trauma.

Lesson introduction

As we think of the suffering we have experienced, it is helpful to look beyond our own lives to our family and group history. Trauma and blessing are both handed down from one generation to the next. To address these roots, we need to uncover them.

1. Danielle's story (15 min)

Danielle had known hard times. But life had gotten a little better since the country's unrest had quieted down. The town she lived in felt more peaceful and the nearby city was being rebuilt. New government officials seemed to want to help the people recover. Danielle had cautious hope of new beginnings and believed that starting a family with her husband James would bring back some of the closeness that they had felt when they had first gotten married a few years earlier.

After several heartbreaking miscarriages, Danielle gave birth to twins, Sarah and Philip. The birth of the twins brought joy to Danielle's heart. She had hoped that James would begin to spend more time at home. Back when uncertainty began increasing in their country, it had been nice to care for and support each other. But since James had returned from serving in the military, it seems he had forgotten what they used to share. His time in the military had changed him. He rarely smiled and often spent evenings away from home, often drinking to numb the pain. James had a hard time finding work and when he did, his habits often caused him to lose his job.

Danielle took on a lot of the responsibility of providing for the family by working hard as a seamstress. As a little girl, she remembers watching her mother work long hours into the night sewing to support the family. Her father had died in an uprising in their town shortly after she was born. Danielle had heard stories from her older siblings about how her father was not often home but her mother never spoke of these things.

Danielle did the best she could to provide safety and love for her children, but there was very little peace in their home. Like her mother, Danielle remained silent about her pain and losses. There were many evenings where James yelled at Danielle then left the house. By the time Sarah and Philip were teenagers, there had been many evenings that they went to bed scared, confused, and unable to fall asleep. Although Danielle felt tired and sad most of the time, she found that caring for her children gave her purpose. Danielle and the kids attended church on Sundays. They found some rest and comfort here. James never joined them.

Sarah and Philip were able to complete school, but Sarah had more difficulty than her brother because she often found it very hard to focus. Danielle desperately wanted to help her children have a better future and so she saved enough money over the years to send both of them to university in the city.

The siblings lived together during university. Philip began his studies with great interest and motivation. He remembered how hard his mother worked and wanted to make her proud. He spent most of his time going to class and studying. On Sundays, he continued to attend church.

16

Sarah was not doing well with her studies. She found it difficult to focus and had trouble concentrating. She was enjoying living in the city; it was new and exciting. Philip tried talking to her about his concerns but she refused to listen and finally moved out on her own.

After graduating, Philip was able to get a good job. When their father died, Sarah did not attend the funeral. She had stopped answering calls and emails and no one in the family had any contact with her. Both Philip and Danielle prayed that one day they might be reunited with Sarah.

Then one day, Philip received a call from Sarah who sounded frantic and said she was at a hospital nearby. In the background, he could hear a child crying. Sarah said that she could not return to her boyfriend because he had just hit their 2-year-old daughter, Abigail, who was being treated for a broken arm. "Philip, I don't know what to do. Can you please help us to be safe?"

SMALL GROUP DISCUSSION

1. What contributed to the difficulties that James and Danielle experienced?
2. How were Sarah and Philip impacted by their parents?
3. What strengths may have been passed down through the generations? What challenges?

2. What is generational trauma and blessing? (30 min)

Generational trauma is trauma that is passed from one generation to the next. For example, addictions, domestic violence, racism, and prejudice are often passed on from parent to child. Generational blessing is the blessing that children inherit from their parents. This can include strong faith in God, integrity, emotional well-being, economic well-being, and hope for the future (*Exodus 20:4-6*).

Generational trauma can be passed on:

- through what is taught and modeled in a family and society.
- from mother to child during pregnancy.

LARGE GROUP DISCUSSION

How might each of the reactions to trauma listed below affect a person's ability to parent?

1. Reliving a traumatic experience
2. Avoiding pain by avoiding feeling any emotion, being distant, using painkillers (drugs, alcohol, medications)
3. Being on alert all the time, tense, afraid

Share feedback in the large group and then add anything from below that has not already been mentioned:

- If we grow up in a caring, strong family, it is easier to have an inner strength.
- If we grow up in a home that is not safe, we risk passing on the pain and insecurity to our children and the cycle continues.
- We may not understand why we continue to experience painful emotions.
- Even in difficult cases, there is hope.
- Children who have experienced trauma can heal, even with just one caring adult in their lives.

Activity: Making a family tree[4]

To explore generational trauma and blessing in your family, make a family tree. The example in Figure 7 shows Danielle's family tree for four generations.

- Use a pencil when you make your family tree, since you may need to erase and adjust as you go.
- You may not know all of your relatives, but include as many as you know, alive or dead. If you do not know many of your relatives, include people who are "like family" to you. As you find out more about your family, you can add to this family tree.
- Decide which generations you will include. The example of Danielle's family includes 4 generations, but it does not include the generations earlier than her mother. Make a row for each generation. Start by putting yourself in the appropriate row in your family.
- A horizontal line between two people shows marriage. If a man has more than one spouse, put several diagonal lines from the man, starting with the first wife on the left. Put a vertical line down from a marriage to show the children, from oldest on top to youngest. Put an X through anyone who is deceased.

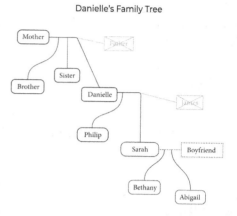

Danielle's Family Tree

Figure 7. Family tree example

DISCUSSION IN TWOS

What did you find helpful or difficult in this activity?

Share Feedback

Now that you have drawn your family tree, in the next section we will consider sources of trauma and blessing that may have affected family members through the generations.

---

3. Identifying generational trauma and blessing (20 min)

In *Healing the Wounds of Trauma*, there are three questions that help us listen to people tell their story of trauma: 1) What happened? 2) How did you feel? And 3) What was the hardest part? When looking at generational trauma, you may need to do some research to answer the first question, "What happened?"

LARGE GROUP DISCUSSION

Why might it be difficult to find out about your family's history?

Share feedback in the large group and then add anything from below that has not already been mentioned:

- Often families hide shameful experiences. We may think we know everything about our family members, and then a family secret comes out—for example, an uncle who you thought died of an illness actually took his own life.
- There is no record of what happened in earlier generations.
- People may be separated and have lost contact with each other.

---

[4]Facilitator: Be available to help people work on their family trees. If it brings up too much pain for anyone, encourage him/her to take a break. Reassure them there is hope even if their family has passed on trauma.

Activity: Identifying generational trauma and blessing

Look at your family tree and think about each person. Did anyone in your family experience trauma? Read the list below and write the word or abbreviation of the word next to the name of anyone who experienced that kind of trauma. Add any other traumas that come to mind for your family.

Addiction   Divorce/separation   Mental illness
Domestic abuse   Sexual abuse   Disability
Sudden death   Infidelity   Chronic illness
Suicide   Polygamy   Poverty
Prison   Kidnapped

Now think about the important blessings family members have passed on. Read the list below and write the word or abbreviation of the word next to the name of anyone who passed on that kind of blessing. Add any other blessings that come to mind for your family.

Honesty   Faith in God   Kindness
Courage   Faithfulness in marriage Patience
Laughter   Wealth   Education

DISCUSSION IN TWOS

1. Do you notice any patterns of trauma being passed on from generation to generation in your family? Explain.
2. Do you notice any patterns of blessing being passed on from generation to generation in your family? Explain.
3. Is there information you are lacking about your family? How does that make you feel?
4. What are you passing on to the next generation?

4. Generational trauma and blessing in the Bible (15 min)

What does the Bible say about generational trauma and blessing?

SMALL GROUP DISCUSSION

Read *Exodus 34:6–7* and *Jeremiah 18:7-10*.

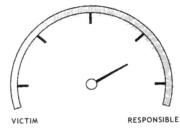

Figure 8. Responsibility meter

1. Do you think God punishes us for the sins of our grandparents, or does he hold us responsible for the choices we make? How do you put these passages together?
2. Where do you think people fall on the 'responsibility meter': How much are we victims of our family's heritage, and how much are we responsible for the choices we make?
3. Where do you place yourself on this 'responsibility meter' at this time?

- Cycles of generational trauma continue until they are broken.
- The good news is that, with effort, cycles can be broken!
- We can choose to do good and stop the cycle of pain.
- There is no evil that God cannot redeem.
- Joseph chose to change the pattern in his family. He told his brothers, "Do not be upset or blame yourselves because you sold me here. It was really God who sent me ahead of you to save people's lives . . . God sent me ahead of you to rescue you in this amazing way and to make sure that you and your descendants survive" (*Genesis 45:5, 7*).
- Even when people have done harmful things, God is at work.

5. Responding to generational trauma (15 min)

Patterns of generational trauma were not formed in a day, and they will not be overcome in a day. They need to be addressed emotionally, physically, spiritually and economically. Little by little, with consistent dedication, entire families can become healthy.

SMALL GROUP DISCUSSION

1. What steps can you take to heal from generational trauma?
2. What steps can you take to help your family recognize and stop patterns of trauma?

Share feedback in the large group and then add anything from below that has not already been mentioned:

- Pray that your family can break the cycle of trauma.
- Talk together.
  - Create safe spaces for conversation where family members can become aware of the patterns of trauma.
  - Listen to one another's stories.
  - Do research to find out about your family, if it helps.
- Grieve your family's losses.
  - Grieve any family members that are missing.
  - Allow yourself to weep for your family, for the pain passed down from one generation to the next. When Joseph reunited with his family, he wept so loudly people outside could hear him (*Genesis 45:1–2*).
  - Write a lament.
- Take the pain of your family to Jesus. Help family members know Jesus, who bore our pain on the cross. Where there is life, there is hope (*2 Corinthians 5:17-19*).
- Forgive those who caused pain.
- Reconcile with family members when possible.
- Celebrate the family's strengths and those who have been good examples to follow.
- Think about how you might contribute to a legacy of blessing.

6. Closing exercise (10 min)

Trauma has an impact across generations, but we can also remember the blessings we have enjoyed and the people that have been examples to us.

Remembering our blessings

Read *Joshua 4:1–7* outloud.

God had the Israelites make a rock memorial so that they could remind themselves and their children of how God saved them from their enemies by drying up the Jordan so they could pass through on dry ground.

Think about God's goodness to you and your family. Who in your family has been an anchor, a pillar? If not in your family, is there someone who is like family to you that has been a source of strength? How can you remind yourself of that person so that you remember God's faithfulness amidst pain? Some options are:

- Put a photo of that person in your house or as a screen saver on your phone or computer.
- Write or paint their name on a stone. Put this stone in a place you will see often.
- Make a drawing, painting or collage that shows what this person means to you.
- Think of another way that works in your context.

As a group pray, thanking God for these people and praying for your families.

Lesson 4. Shame and guilt

Before you begin:

- This lesson will likely take more than 1 ½ hours. You may want to break it into two sessions, doing Sections 1-3 in one and Sections 4-7 in another.
- For Section 2: Prepare slips of paper with the shame/guilt statements.
- For Section 4: Prepare a chart on flip chart for comparison of biblical and cultural understandings of honor and shame.
- For Section 5: Prepare slips of paper with Bible verses.

In this lesson we will:

- Explore the characteristics of shame and guilt.
- Identify similarities and differences between cultural and biblical principles of shame.
- Discover ways that we can heal from shame and guilt both as individuals and as the church.

Lesson introduction

When we experience trauma—whether our own or generational—we may also experience shame and guilt. How are these the same and different? And more importantly, how can we heal from shame and guilt?

1. Shame and guilt in the Garden of Eden (10 min)

God created the universe and placed Adam and Eve in the Garden of Eden. Of all the animals God made, the snake was the most cunning. The snake asked the woman, "Did God really tell you not to eat fruit from any tree in the garden?"

"We may eat the fruit of any tree in the garden," the woman answered, "except the tree in the middle of it. God told us not to eat the fruit of that tree or even touch it; if we do, we will die."

The snake replied, "That's not true; you will not die. God said that, because he knows that when you eat it, you will be like God and know what is good and what is bad."

The woman saw how beautiful the tree was and how good its fruit would be to eat, and she thought how wonderful it would be to become wise. So she took some of the fruit and ate it. Then she gave some to her husband, and he also ate it. As soon as they had eaten it, they realized that they were naked, so they sewed fig leaves together and covered themselves.

That evening they heard the LORD God walking in the garden, and they hid from him among the trees. But the LORD God called out to the man, "Where are you?"

He answered, "I heard you in the garden. I was afraid and hid from you, because I was naked."

"Who told you that you were naked?" God asked. "Did you eat the fruit that I told you not to eat?"

The man answered, "The woman you put here with me gave me the fruit, and I ate it."

The LORD God asked the woman, "Why did you do this?"

She replied, "The snake tricked me into eating it."

(Based on Genesis 1–3)

SMALL GROUP DISCUSSION

1. What were Adam and Eve guilty of? What were they ashamed of?
2. How did they respond to their shame and guilt?
3. How did God respond to them?

Share feedback in the large group.

2. What are shame and guilt? (15 min)

We often experience shame and guilt together, but they are separate emotions. The better we understand them, the better we can respond to them.

Small Group Activity

1. Write these phrases on separate slips of paper. Give each small group a set.

    I did something bad. I broke a law or rule.
    I am bad, inadequate, inferior.
    I fear being punished.
    I fear being abandoned.
    I can do something to fix this.
    I just want to hide or disappear.

2. On two large papers, write the words "Shame" and "Guilt".
3. Have each person take a slip, read it aloud, and put it on the paper that it is most connected with, guilt or shame. If there is a difference of opinion, discuss it and try to come to a consensus.
4. Look at the slips on each paper and summarize your definition of shame contrasted to guilt.

In the large group, go over the slips and discuss responses.[5] Add anything from below not already mentioned:

Guilt says, "I did something bad." Shame says, "I am bad." Shame is the feeling of falling short, not being good enough (*Romans 3:23*).

Feelings of shame and guilt can range from mild to severe. For example, our feeling of shame may range from feeling slightly embarrassed to feeling completely despicable.

We may feel ashamed of ourselves, or people may shame us.

When we feel shame, we try to hide. When we feel guilt, we try to find a way to remedy the situation if we can. If not, we may feel regret.

If we have done something we consider wrong, we may feel both shame and guilt. But sometimes we can feel shame without feeling guilt. This happens when we suffer for things we did not choose, for example, being short or being abused. It can also happen for things we feel are right like speaking the truth or defending someone who is weak, and others criticize, ridicule or persecute us for it.

SMALL GROUP DISCUSSION

Think of, or read, the stories of the woman with the issue of blood (*Luke 8:43-48*) and the woman caught in adultery (*John 8:1-11*).

1. Which woman do you think felt shame?
2. Which woman do you think felt both guilt and shame?

Both shame and guilt are painful emotions, but are they harmful or helpful?

SMALL GROUP DISCUSSION

1. Think of times when you felt shame:
    a. Were there ways shame helped you become a better person?
    b. Were there ways shame hindered you from becoming a better person?
2. Think of times when you felt guilt:
    a. Were there ways guilt helped you become a better person?
    b. Were there ways guilt hindered you from becoming a better person?

Suggested response: Shame: I am bad, inadequate, inferior. I fear being abandoned. I just want to hide or disappear. Guilt: I did something bad. I broke a law or rule. I fear being punished. I can do something to fix this. (It is not necessary to agree on every detail. Discussion helps us grasp the concepts.)

Helpful

God gave us the painful feelings of shame and guilt to alert us to things we should pay attention to. These emotions are like the nerve endings in our hands that let us know when we are too close to fire and risk getting burned.

It can be helpful to feel guilt when we have done things we consider wrong or dishonorable.

If we never experience guilt, we may have problems like the people in the time of Jeremiah who did things they should have been ashamed of, but "they did not know how to blush" (*Jeremiah 6:15*).

Harmful

Shame and guilt can be harmful when we did not have any choice in what happened.

We call this 'false' shame or guilt because the feelings are sending a false alert to us: something has been imposed on us we don't have control over.

We cannot correct it.

For example, we may feel 'false shame':

- for the way our body looks, or the kind of family we were born into.
- for being the victim of rape, domestic abuse, or being displaced.
- for our language, ethnicity, race, or way of life (*1 Peter 4:3-5*).

We can also feel 'false guilt' about things we did not have control over, for example:

- for surviving a disaster when others died in it.
- for doing things that were forced on us by others or by circumstances, like killing someone in self-defense.
- if we are accused falsely, even though we know we have done nothing wrong.

Whatever the source of our shame or guilt, it is our response that matters. Where we need to repent, we can do so. There is no condemnation for those in Christ (*Romans 8:1*). Even helpful shame or guilt can be harmful if we refuse to accept God's forgiveness for our sins and let those feelings go. Where we have nothing to repent of, we can rest in God's love for us (*2 Corinthians 7:10*).[6]

---

4. Cultures and the Bible (15 min)

Different cultures give honor and shame to different things. For example, in some cultures, being loyal to family members is considered honorable even if it means lying to those outside the family. In other cultures, telling the truth is more honorable than being loyal to family members.

SMALL GROUP DISCUSSION

Fill out the chart below, either with everyone answering all the questions or dividing them up between groups. What are some things:

- your culture considers honorable?
- your culture considers shameful?

- that God considers honorable?
- that God considers shameful?

	Honorable	Shameful
Culture		
God		

God's Word helps us know what is honorable and shameful in his eyes. For example, a mother who reports that her child was raped may be accused by the community of exposing someone who did a shameful act, but in God's eyes children are of great value and deserve to be protected from molesters. Or, many cultures shame

[Optional Small Group Challenge (30 min): Read one or more of these passages. Who was shamed? What was considered guilt? Who was responsible for the shame or guilt? How did the people respond? David and Bathsheba in *2 Samuel 12:1-13* and *Psalm 51*; The lost sons in *Luke 15:11-27*; Hannah in *1 Samuel 1:1-8*; Hagar in *Genesis 16; 21:1-20*.

24

a woman who has been raped, but in God's eyes, it is the rapist who should be ashamed. We need to study God's Word and let it shape what we consider shameful and honorable.

5. How can we find healing for shame and guilt? (25 min)

Shame goes inside us and becomes a part of how we see ourselves, while guilt is more about external acts. Because of this, it is harder to find healing from shame than from guilt. The good news is that, with God's help, there is healing for both shame and guilt.

DISCUSSION IN TWOS

Share as much as you feel comfortable with one another about the questions below.

1. In times when you have felt shame:

    Did anything reduce your shame? If yes, what?
    Did anything increase your shame? If yes, what?

2. In times when you have felt guilt:

    Did anything reduce your feeling of guilt? If yes, what?
    Did anything increase your feeling of guilt? If yes, what?

The Bible shows us how we can heal from shame and guilt.

SMALL GROUP DISCUSSION

1. What do these verses tell us about finding healing for shame and guilt?
    James 5:16
    2 Corinthians 7:9-10
    Ephesians 5:11
    1 John 1:5-9

2. What happens when we tell our story to others?
    Psalm 133
    1 Peter 1:22
    John 17:22-23a
    Hebrews 10:23-25

3. How does Jesus' death on the cross help us heal from our shame and guilt?
    Isaiah 53:3-5
    1 Peter 2:24
    Hebrews 12:2b
    Philippians 2:5-8

Share feedback in the large group and then add anything from below that has not already been mentioned:

Tell our story to others. As we learned in *Healing the Wounds of Trauma*, we need to tell our shameful secret to trustworthy people who care and listen well (*James 5:16a*). We may fear others will abandon us or cause us further pain if they knew our secret. In fact, fellowship deepens as we share our suffering (*1 John 1:5-9; Philippians 3:10*). Being honest may give others the courage to be honest. And it helps us be honest with ourselves and know ourselves. And the better we know ourselves, the better we can experience being known by God. We do not need to keep secrets from God.

Figure 9. Knowing self, God, and other

If we have sinned, we can repent and ask God and others to forgive us and accept that forgiveness (*2 Corinthians 7:10*). If we are suffering from false guilt or false shame, we begin to remove its power over us by exposing it (*Ephesians 5:11*).

Live in community. We were created for community (*Genesis 2:18*), and fellowship brings us joy (*Psalm 133; 1 Peter 1:22; John 17:22*). Together we can strengthen our faith about what is honorable and good so we can stand up against the pressures of society (*Hebrews 10:23–25*). When we embrace what God considers honorable, we are able to resist 'false' shame others try to impose on us. Jesus gives us the example on the cross: "For the joy set before him he endured the cross, scorning its shame, and sat down at the right hand of the throne of God" (*Hebrews 12:2; see also Philippians 2:1–11; Hebrews 13:12–14*).

Even if others try to shame us, it is what God honors that really matters (*1 Corinthians 1:27*) and, in the end, God honors those who follow him. For example, Joseph endured many shameful situations, like being sold into slavery, being falsely accused of sexual harassment, being thrown into prison. But each time, God raised him up and restored his honor.

Look to Jesus as our healer and our example. Jesus took our shame and guilt on himself on the cross (*Isaiah 53*). We can bring our shame and guilt to him without hiding any part of ourselves. His death restores our honor and innocence (*Psalm 31:1; Isaiah 6:1*). Our response is to praise God for this mercy.

---

6. How can the church restore honor and dignity? (10 min)

The church has an important role in helping people heal from shame and guilt.

SMALL GROUP DISCUSSION

In church or ministry groups, think about these questions:

1. How much is your church or ministry a place where people can tell one another their real problems?
2. How does your church or ministry respond to people who are going through shameful situations? If they are innocent? If they are responsible?
3. What has your church or ministry done to honor people that society stigmatizes?

Share feedback in the large group and add anything from below not already mentioned:

The church can create an atmosphere of grace where it is safe to talk about personal issues and be fully known by others. (Church leaders may need to share with other church leaders.)

The church can help people learn how to listen and keep things confidential.

The church can reach out to those who are experiencing shame or guilt. Even when people have done bad things, like murder, they should not only be known for the bad thing they have done. If a church practices excommunication, it should be done with the intent of restoring the person back into fellowship with God and others (*Matthew 18:17*).

The church can hold up what is good and honorable according to God's standards (*Matthew 5:1–12*). We need to repeat these things often (*Hebrews 10:25*).

The church can reach out to groups shamed by society. For example, Mother Teresa helped poor people of Calcutta die in dignity. Actions like this send a message that all people are created in the image of God and have value (*Genesis 1:26–27; Ephesians 4:32*). The church can help restore their dignity.

7. Closing exercise (10 min)

We are not alone in our shame. Get quiet inside and listen: Is there any burden of guilt or shame you would like to bring to God? All of us are capable of doing bad things. We do not need to hide any part of ourselves from God like Adam and Eve first did in the garden. By bringing these burdens to God in prayer, he can heal us and restore us to a right relationship with himself.

Lesson 5. Using our feelings for good

Before you begin:

- For Section 2: Print 4 copies of the skit.
    - Will need a large cloth or sheet for the skit.
- For Section 3: Each group of people will need 8-10 slips of paper that they can write on.
- For Section 4: Each person will need a large paper for drawing a body outline.

In this lesson we will:

- Describe how trauma affects our minds and feelings.
- Learn to appreciate the role that feelings play in our lives.
- Give examples of how feelings can be used for good or bad.
- Begin to discern how our feelings affect our bodies.
- Begin to overcome patterns of negative responses.
- Practice using our feelings to draw closer to God.

Lesson introduction

Long after we have begun to heal from a traumatic experience, we may still find it difficult to manage our feelings. Big or small things may remind us of the trauma and set off an emotional reaction so strong we feel out of control. Part of the long journey of healing is to learn to identify our feelings and use their energy for good. We can even use them to know God better.

---

1. Simon's accident (20 min)

One evening Simon was going home from work on his motorbike. Suddenly, as he turned a corner, he heard a big bang. A large truck was coming towards him, swaying from side to side.

Simon swerved frantically to avoid the truck, but one wheel caught his bike and threw him off on the grassy roadside. As he lay there in a daze, there was another enormous sound as the truck crashed across the road. The next thing he knew a car was driving up and people were getting out. They helped to get the driver out of the truck, but they saw it was too late: the driver was dead. One of the men saw Simon lying at the side of the road and rushed to help him.

The men took Simon to the nearest hospital. As he lay on his hospital bed, his thoughts went in circles. "My leg hurts so much. Will I lose it? Will anyone think it was my fault the truck crashed? Why has God let this happen? What will my wife say? Will I be able to work again?"

Two weeks later Simon was back home with his leg in plaster. The doctor assured him that the leg would heal; he just had to be patient. He was feeling relieved but also frustrated that he could not get around easily. He was also worried that he might lose his job. Sometimes his pain and frustration made him get irritated at his wife.

Three months later the whole experience had become like a bad dream. He looked normal again and everyone expected him to get on with life as though nothing had happened.

SMALL GROUP DISCUSSION

1. What made it difficult for Simon to recover from this trauma?
2. Can you think of a traumatic experience where you were expected to get on with life as though nothing happened? How did you react?

Share feedback in the large group.

2. How our brains work

God made us wonderfully complex (*Psalm 139:14*) with ways to cope in times of high stress. Understanding how our brains function helps us understand why we behave the way we do after trauma. We can use our hand to represent our brain, which has three parts.

- The **reflex** part of our brain keeps our body functioning automatically. It also tells us when we are in danger and automatically activates our body to respond. All our responses go through this part of our brain.

- The **feeling** part of our brain handles our emotions. It helps us process all of the things we are exposed to (sights, smells, sounds, tastes).

- The **thinking** part of our brain helps us organize all this incoming information and manage our emotions so we can respond well.

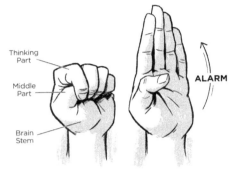

Figure 10. How our brains work

Normally, these three parts of our minds work together, and all is well. But in times of stress, there is no time to think. The thinking part of our brain is overwhelmed and, like a computer with too much information, it goes offline. We can think of the thinking part of our brain flipping its lid, like a pot of water boiling so much the lip flips off. The reflex part of our brain takes over and we respond quickly and automatically in one of three ways:

1. Fight: we attack
2. Flight: we run
3. Freeze: we can't move or respond

This normal response to stress helps us survive emergencies. However, it can lead to two problems:

- We may be triggered by a similar event. For example, if we have lived through war, when we hear fireworks, our feeling brain and reflex brain may take over, even though there is no real danger. A certain smell our feeling brain associates with abuse may make us panic. This can lead to confusion and shame.
- If we are on alert all the time, ready to respond to a crisis even when there is no crisis, we will wear our bodies out.

Act out this skit:

Simon visits the pastor

You will need:

☐ Actors seated or standing in a row:

> A Reflex Brain actor
> A Feeling Brain actor
> A Thinking Brain actor
> A pastor

☐ Props: A sheet or large cloth held up between Feeling Brain and Thinking Brain.

☐ Sound effect: something to make a loud noise

Scene 1: Simon is chatting with his pastor about the day. Reflex Brain is pumping blood as it should (pumps with arms). Feeling Brain is feeling good about the pleasant moment (smells, smiles, hears sounds). Thinking Brain is talking about plans for the church ministry.

Scene 2: There is a sudden loud noise. Thinking Brain jumps to his feet, screams, and then crawls under his chair to hide. The pastor only sees Thinking Brain, and thinks this is strange behavior. But the audience sees Reflex Brain sounding the alarm, "Danger! Danger! Run!" Feeling Brain says, "I'm so afraid! Oh no! It's happening all over again! I'm so afraid!"

The pastor is quite confused!

1. Have you ever seen someone respond with a fight, flight, or freeze response? Or have you ever responded in any of these ways? Explain.
2. How do people respond to someone who reacts this way?

Share feedback in the large group.

---

3. Feelings: Good or bad? (15 min)

Do you think feelings are good or bad? Or are certain feelings good while others are bad?

Small Group Exercise

1. Write these emotions on slips of paper: love, hate, fear, anger, sorrow, hope, jealousy, joy. Do you usually think of these feelings as good or bad? Sort them into two piles: the good and the bad.
2. Now take the "bad feelings" pile. In what situations could these feelings be considered good?
3. Take the "good feelings" pile. In what situations could these feelings be considered bad?
4. Do you try to avoid certain feelings or feel guilty if you have them? Explain.
5. Read Ecclesiastes 3:1-8 and discuss what it says about emotions.

Share feedback in the large group and then add anything from below that has not already been mentioned:

As human beings, we are created to have all sorts of feelings: happy, sad, peaceful, angry, anxious, afraid and more. Ecclesiastes 3:1–8 tells us there is a time for everything: for sorrow and joy, mourning and dancing, love and hate. No feeling is bad in itself.

---

4. Becoming more aware of our feelings (20 min)

Our bodies can give us clues about how we are feeling even if our brain isn't aware. For example, we may begin sweating, or having cold feet, or a pounding pulse. Our feelings are telling us something. Are we listening?

Activity: Feelings in your body[7]

Take out the body outline paper.

1. Think of a time when you were angry. Where did you feel it in your body? Write "anger" in those places on the body outline.
2. Think of other feelings and mark them on your body outline: fear, joy, sadness, and so forth.
3. Take one of the painful feelings and think of a movement that could help you overcome it. For example, when you are angry, you could stretch, breathe deeply, or take a walk.

In the large group share your drawings and which feelings you experience most often.

---

5. What can we do when we are overwhelmed by strong feelings? (20 min)

Our feelings can be our friend, not our enemy or our master. They give us vitality and guide our choices. They show what is inside our hearts and what we value. As we pay attention to our feelings, we may uncover layers of feelings. For example, under our anger we may find sadness or hurt. This discovery can help us know the source of our pain so we can heal. In this way, we can use our feelings for good.

---

[7]Alternative Activity: Feelings Floor Plan
1. Draw your feelings as if they were a floor plan for a house. Give more space to ones you feel strongly, or that you feel often.
2. Share your floor plan with another person and discuss what you realized about yourself.

SMALL GROUP DISCUSSION

Read these passages.

> *Mark 12:30*
> *Romans 12:2*

1. What challenges have you experienced putting these verses into practice, especially when you are overwhelmed with strong feelings?
2. How can you work with your feelings to grow as a person?

Share feedback in the large group and then add anything from below that has not already been mentioned:

Pay attention to your feelings. Accept them without judging them as bad. If you have no feelings at all, that is actually a more serious problem.

Try to understand where the feeling is coming from. What just happened? What were you thinking about? What is your feeling telling you? What can you learn from it?

Identify any lies, either lies others tell you or lies you tell yourself. Find a short Bible passage or truth that addresses that lie that you can repeat whenever the painful feeling begins. For example, if you feel worthless, you might repeat "God loves me."

If you begin to feel overwhelmed by strong feelings:

Remind yourself that the trauma is over and you are safe, provided this is true. "This is not that."

Use your senses to stay connected to the present. Be aware of what is around you. Breathe deeply and slowly. Move around, go outside, or have a drink of water or tea.

The faucet exercise: Imagine your feelings are in a water tank with a faucet. You can open the faucet and let them out a little bit, and then shut the faucet when you wish.

Find someone you can talk with or draw a picture.

SMALL GROUP DISCUSSION

What do you do when you are overwhelmed by strong emotions?

When is a good time to let the tap open? With whom?

Figure 11. Controlling your emotions like a faucet

Share feedback in the large group.

---

6. Closing activity: Using your feelings to draw closer to God (15 min)

Our feelings can help us experience God more fully, too. For centuries, Christians around the world have used this exercise to let their feelings guide them to know God better.

1. **Individually:** Think back over the past day. List the things that you did.
   a. When did you feel closer to God? What were you doing? Write this down.
   b. When did you feel farther from God? What were you doing? Write this down.

2. **In twos:** Share something that made you feel closer to God, and something that made you feel farther from God.

Do this every day. Try to do more of the things that made you feel closer to God, and fewer of the things that made you feel farther from him.

Close the time by reading *Philippians 4:8-9* aloud.

Lesson 6. Difficult conversations

Before you begin:

- For sections 1 and 3: Choose a strong reader to read the stories.
- For section 4: Provide paper for small groups to record their guidelines.

In this lesson we will:

- Identify what types of conversation can be difficult.
- Begin to recognize our own reactions to difficult conversations.
- Explore the consequences of avoiding difficult conversations.
- Practice ways to lead difficult conversations more successfully.

Lesson introduction

Trauma can isolate people from each other and destroy relationships. For individuals to heal, relationships with family and community also need to heal. For healing to happen, we may need to have difficult conversations—for example, when we need to resolve a conflict, ask for forgiveness, make an apology, or make a difficult decision. Knowing how to address difficult conversations more successfully is a basic skill that helps us live in harmony with others.

1. David has a problem (15 min)

David lived with his wife Lucia, his mother Sarah, and his bachelor brother John Mark in their village compound. Next door lived Samuel with his wife Anne and their family. Their farms were next to each other, too, about two miles from the village. The two families had lived together for generations.

David noticed that Samuel had put in new boundary stones on the edge of his farm and taken a part of the farm David thought was his. He felt irritated by this but didn't want to talk about it with Samuel, so he just complained to his wife and friends about what had happened. When he saw Samuel, he avoided the subject.

After a few weeks, David saw some healthy corn growing tall on the part of the land that Samuel had taken, and this made him feel even more angry. He began to go out of his way to avoid contact with Samuel.

The wives continued to be friendly with each other. Whenever Anne brought up the subject of the farm dispute, Lucia said it wasn't a problem and changed the subject.

David's brother John Mark worked in a computer firm in the nearby town. He was irritated by the problem and went directly to Samuel and said, "Why did you do this? We know exactly where our farm boundaries are!" When Samuel tried to answer, John Mark repeated what he had said even louder, and rode off on his motorbike. He felt happy that he had addressed the issue.

Mother Sarah saw everything that was going on. She didn't want this situation to sour the relationship between the two families. One day she invited Samuel and his family to her house to discuss the issue. After greetings and drinks, she spoke about some of the good times their families had shared, going back for generations. She said to Samuel, "Do you remember how my father and your grandfather started our church?"

After talking about their long history together, she brought up the farm situation and asked Samuel to explain what he thought had happened. Samuel explained that he had found a paper from his father that marked the boundaries of the farm. Then Sarah said, "It shocked David when you put down new boundary stones, because he has a paper, too, and his has different boundaries!" Samuel replied, "How could my grandfather have marked the wrong boundaries?" Sarah agreed that the knowledge of the elders was very important.

Finally, Sarah said, "Would it be good if you and David went together to the land office and see if they have a map that marks the boundaries of the farms? One of my friends at church told me their family dispute was settled by looking at the official map."

"That's a good idea," said Samuel. "Would you talk to David so that we can arrange a day to do this?"

"Gladly," said Sarah.

SMALL GROUP DISCUSSION

1. Describe how David, Lucia, John Mark, and Sarah reacted to this situation[8]
2. When there is a difficult situation, how do you react? Which of the characters in the story are you most like?

Share feedback in the large group.

2. What is a difficult conversation? (10 min)

A conversation can be difficult if:

1. The outcome affects people a lot.
2. People have strong feelings about it.
3. People have different opinions about it.

A difficult conversation may happen when we are resolving a conflict, asking for forgiveness, making an apology, or making a difficult decision as a group.

LARGE OR SMALL GROUP DISCUSSION

In the Bible stories below:

1. Why were these difficult conversations? Use the criteria above.
2. Was the conversation successful or unsuccessful?
   - Gamaliel: *Acts 5:33–40*
   - The clerk at the riot in *Ephesus: Acts 19:28–29, 35–41*

Share feedback in the large group.

---

3. Avoiding difficult conversations: Causes and consequences (15 min)

We may find ourselves avoiding difficult conversations and suffer the consequences. King David did just that in this story.

King David had several wives and many children. David favored Amnon, his firstborn son who was in line for the throne. Absalom was his third son by a different wife, and Tamar was Absalom's beautiful sister.

Amnon fell in love with his half-sister Tamar. He tricked her to come into his bedroom and raped her there. Suddenly his love turned to hate and he threw her out. She wept inconsolably and tore her robe in grief.

When David heard about what Amnon had done, he was very angry but he did not do anything because Amnon was his favorite son.

When Absalom heard what had happened, he was incensed. He took Tamar into his home. He hated Amnon so much he never spoke to him again.

Two years later, Absalom arranged a way to have Amnon killed. Then he had to run for his life to another country to escape his father's anger. He stayed there for three years. Finally, David called for him to come back to Jerusalem. But even then, David refused to see him.

Absalom was bitter against David and tried to take the throne from him. He died in the attempt. This made King David even sadder.

(Based on *2 Samuel 13* ff.)

---

[8]David avoided talking with Samuel altogether, Lucia changed the subject if it came up, John Mark talked but did not listen, Sarah helped them remember their shared history, rebuilt trust, and helped them listen to each other's perspective and identify a next step to address the issue.

1. Why do you think David avoided having a difficult conversation with Amnon? What are some other reasons people avoid difficult conversations?

2. What were the consequences for David of avoiding the difficult conversation? What are some other consequences of avoiding difficult conversations?

Share feedback in the large group and then add anything from below that has not already been mentioned about the reasons people generally avoid difficult conversations and the consequences:

We may avoid difficult conversations for many reasons:

- Practice: Lacking practice needed to address issues more successfully.
- Power differences: It may not be socially acceptable to address the issue.
- Culture: Our culture may not encourage us to address difficult issues.
- Risky: Our relationship may get worse if the person responds negatively. Or we may be punished by those with political, social, or mystical power.
- Time: It takes time and we feel we are too busy to bother.
- If we avoid difficult conversations, our church, ministry, family, or organization will suffer.
- The list of "topics to avoid" may become so long that we live in a culture of silence. Everyone may feel nervous lest these topics be brought up.
- Issues are not resolved because they cannot be discussed.
- There may be division, backbiting, frustration, or anger, either expressed or under the surface. This may result in revolt or violence.
- Little wounds may fester into big sores. In the same way, small misunderstandings may lead to broken relationships and even cause generational trauma.
- People may lose respect for one another.

DISCUSSION IN TWOS

It can be hard to know whether or not you should address a difficult issue or let it pass. Think about a time when you had to decide whether to address a difficult issue or let it pass.

1. What factors helped you decide?
2. How did you feel about it afterwards?

Share feedback in the large group.

---

4. How can we lead difficult conversations more successfully? (45 min)

We many not always succeed in resolving difficult issues, but we can always try to improve our skills in addressing them. This will help us live at peace with others (*Romans 15:5*). It is not necessarily what you say that hurts people, it's how you say it (*Proverbs 15:1*). If people feel safe and respected, you can address any topic.

Cultures differ in how they approach difficult conversations. This is true of different cultures represented in the Bible. For example, in Genesis people use intermediaries (*Genesis 32:3–5*), while in Matthew people are encouraged to go to the person directly (*Matthew 18:15–17*). Whatever the approach, issues need to be addressed or the problem will continue under the surface and cause trouble.

1. What process does your culture use to handle difficult conversations? Do you use intermediaries, go directly, or have another approach?

2. What guidelines would you recommend people in your culture use to address difficult issues?

Share feedback in the large group and then add anything from the guidelines below that has not already been mentioned:

As you go through the guidelines below, compare them with your guidelines. How are they similar or different?

Prepare for the meeting:

1. Pray for discernment, for the Holy Spirit's intervention, for receptive hearts, and for good outcomes. Search your heart to be sure your motivation is pure.

2. Know the outcome you want most. Know what you want most out of the conversation and keep it clearly in mind. For example, is your priority to find a good solution to the problem or to prove you are right?

3. Get the right people, time, place, and information. Think carefully about who should be involved. Choose the time carefully. Find a safe place for the conversation. Get any information needed for the discussion. Sometimes conflicts are resolved by just having the right information.

At the meeting:

1. **Make it safe.** Sit in a circle. To begin the conversation, talk about things you have in common: shared values, goals, and any history of working together successfully. Communicate your respect for people, both with words and your body language. Be prepared to learn things you were not aware of. Be attentive to what the people are communicating, both with words and body language. For example, silence may mean someone does not feel safe.

   Whenever you notice someone starting to leave the circle, either physically or mentally, stop talking about the issue and return to talking about your shared goals, how much the person is valued, and so forth. When the person feels safe again, you can go back to discussing the issue. If people do not feel safe, it may be necessary to stop and set a time to meet again later.

   If you find you want to get out of the circle, remind yourself of your shared goals and your commitment to address the topic.

2. **Tell the story.** Have each person tell the story of what happened from their perspective using these questions:

   What happened?

   What were you thinking about the situation at the time?

   What have you thought about the situation since?

   Who has been affected by what happened? How have they been affected?

   What do you think you could you do to help make things right?

   Tell the story fairly. Don't leave out bits to make yourself look good! Don't judge the motives of others. Everyone should listen until it is their turn to speak.[9]

3. **Agree on next steps.** Agree on next steps if possible, even if you are not able to solve everything in one conversation. You can adjust the plan along the way. Pray together and celebrate that you have begun the conversation.

---

[9]If the issue is a difficult decision that needs to be made, have each person explain:
   1. What is the situation, as you see it?
   2. What are the possible decisions you see?
   3. Who would be affected by each option, and how?
   4. What do you feel is the best decision?

Choose one of the stories below and role play the "difficult conversation" that takes place, using what you have learned in this lesson to complete the skit.

Stolen oranges

Characters:

the boy
Richard and his wife
the boy's parents
their pastor

One day, early in the morning, a man named Richard was in his house, talking with his wife. Through the window, he saw his neighbor's eight-year-old son stealing oranges from his tree. He rushed out, grabbed the child, and started beating him with a hoe he had picked up as he ran. The boy screamed loudly and his parents came running. By the time they got there, the boy was on the ground writhing in pain. The parents rushed him to the hospital. The doctors kept him in the hospital for several days. Finally, he was well enough to be released. The family had to pay a huge medical bill. Both families attended a local church, and their pastor came around one day to try to bring about reconciliation between the families. . .

Dog in the garden

Characters:

Thomas
Ruth
Maurice
Ann
Rusty
the children
the pastor

Thomas and Ruth lived next door to Maurice and Ann in a small town. They all went to the same church and were friends. Maurice and Ann were proud of the vegetables and flowers they grew in their garden.

Thomas and Ruth had two small children and didn't bother much with their yard. One day Thomas and Ruth decided to get a dog from the animal shelter. They came home with a large friendly half-grown mongrel they named Rusty. Soon Rusty was racing around in their garden and playing happily with the children.

Then one morning, Rusty got into Maurice and Ann's yard. He dug up all the tomatoes in their garden and jumped all over the flowers. Maurice grabbed the dog by his collar and dragged him around to Thomas's front door. "Take your dog!" he said, "He's destroyed our garden!" Before Thomas could answer, Maurice marched back to his house.

For the next week, Thomas tried hard to keep the dog under control but one night he got out again, and this time he dug up Ann's favorite roses! From that point on Maurice and Ann refused to speak to Thomas and Ruth, even when they were at church. Now the pastor is trying to help them to be reconciled. . . . .

Lost and found money

Characters:

John
his wife
George
his wife
the pastor.

John finds a $100 bill on the street in front of his house. He puts it in his pocket and begins thinking how he will spend it. Two days later, his wife tells him that their neighbor George is having a problem. He needs medicine for his wife's diabetes, but a $100 bill is missing from his wallet. He has looked everywhere but cannot find it. John begins to feel nervous and afraid. Finally he tells his wife what happened. They discuss what to do and decide to ask their pastor for help. The pastor says they should visit George and his wife for a talk. . . . .

5. Closing activity (5 min)

Reflect on these questions:

1. What difficult conversations might I need to address? With whom?

2. How can I address these? When?

DISCUSSION IN TWOS

 Share your thoughts and pray for each other.
Pray for God's help and blessing as you take this initiative.

Lesson 7. Pursuing reconciliation

Before you begin:

- For section 2: Prepare 5 slips of paper with Bible verses for each table.
- For section 3:
  - Cut 5 large shapes from paper. Write one word from the diagram on each of the shapes. Place 1 shape on each table.
  - Prepare the skit.
- For section 5: Cut 6 large shapes from paper. Write one word from the diagram on each of the shapes. Place 1 shape on each table.

In this lesson we will:

- Explore good ways to talk with people who have hurt us and offer forgiveness.
- Find good ways to approach people we have hurt and ask for forgiveness.

Lesson introduction

We are called to live in harmony with others, but sometimes our relationships are strained. Others may have hurt us, or we may have hurt them. This is a normal part of living in community. We need to use the skills of leading 'difficult conversations' (Lesson 6) to pursue reconciliation: either forgiving others or asking others to forgive us.

---

1. The Lost Sons (10 min)

Jesus told this story:

There was once a man who had two sons. The younger one said to him, "Father, give me my share of the property now." So the man divided his property between his two sons. After a few days the younger son sold his part of the property and left home with the money.

He went to a country far away, where he wasted his money in reckless living. He spent everything he had. Then a severe famine spread over that country, and he was left without anything. So he went to work for one of the citizens of that country, who sent him out to his farm to take care of the pigs. He wished he could fill himself with the bean pods the pigs ate, but no one gave him anything to eat.

At last he came to his senses and said, "All my father's hired workers have more than they can eat, and here I am about to starve! I will get up and go to my father and say, 'Father, I have sinned against God and against you. I am no longer fit to be called your son; treat me as one of your hired workers.'" So he got up and started back to his father.

He was still a long way from home when his father saw him; his heart was filled with pity, and he ran, threw his arms around his son, and kissed him. "Father," the son said, "I have sinned against God and against you. I am no longer fit to be called your son." But the father called his servants. "Hurry!" he said. "Bring the best robe and put it on him. Put a ring on his finger and shoes on his feet. Then go and get the prize calf and kill it and we'll celebrate with a feast! For this son of mine was dead, but now he is alive; he was lost, but now he has been found." And so the feasting began.

In the meantime, the elder son was out in the field. On his way back, when he came close to the house, he heard the music and dancing. So he called one of the servants and asked him, "What's going on?" "Your brother has come back home," the servant answered, "and your father has killed the prize calf, because he got him back safe and sound."

The elder brother was so angry that he would not go into the house; so his father came out and begged him to come in. But he answered his father, "Look, all these years I have worked for you like a slave, and I have never disobeyed your orders. What have you given me? Not even a goat for me to have a feast with my friends! But this son of yours wasted all your property on prostitutes, and when he comes back home, you kill the prize calf for him!"

"My son," the father answered, "you are always here with me, and everything I have is yours. But we had to celebrate and be happy, because your brother was dead, but now he is alive; he was lost, but now he has been found."

(Luke 15:11–32)

SMALL GROUP DISCUSSION

1. Who needed to reconcile with whom?
2. What did each person do to pursue reconciliation?
3. Think of a time when you have felt like one of the sons or like the father.

Share feedback in the large group.

---

2. What attitudes are necessary to live in harmony with others? (15 min)

SMALL GROUP DISCUSSION

Write the word "harmony" in the center of a flip chart paper. Give each group some blank slips of paper. What do these verses say about living at peace with others? Write the attitudes you discover on the slips provided.

Romans 1 2:17-18
Philippians 2:6-11
Romans 15:7
Acts 10:34–45
Matthew 18:15–17
Matthew 5:23-24
Proverbs 9:7-9

Have each group tape their slips on the flip chart around the word harmony. Then add anything from below that has not already been mentioned:

- As much as it is up to us, we need to try to live in peace with everyone—no exceptions.
- God accepts all people equally and forgives us all generously.
- We should have the same attitude as God towards others and offer/ask for forgiveness whenever necessary.
- These are often difficult conversations and the outcome is unpredictable.
- Our offer may be accepted or rejected. Still, we should do our part to live in peace with everybody.

---

3. Offering the gift of forgiveness (30 min)

Healing the Wounds of Trauma helps us bring our pain to Christ and forgive others in our hearts, a process that takes time. When we are ready, we can take the next step in the process.

LARGE GROUP DISCUSSION

1. When is it wise to offer forgiveness to someone who has hurt you?
2. When is it wise to wait to offer forgiveness?
3. When is it wise to forgive someone in your heart without talking to them about it?

In some situations, it is not possible to offer forgiveness to those who have hurt us, either because we cannot contact them or because it would not be safe to do so. In these cases, we can find an alternative, such as writing a letter to the person, telling someone who stands in their place, or telling God in prayer.

Activity

Sally and **Debbie** work in the same office. One day their boss asks them to work together on a project, with Debbie the leader. Debbie is very busy at home and doesn't do much to help Sally. When she gives the completed project to their boss, she does not tell him that Sally did almost all of the work. The boss is so pleased with the work that he offers Debbie a promotion. In the moment, Debbie doesn't know what to do. She knows Sally did the work, but she could use the extra money to pay some unexpected bills, so she smiles and accepts his offer.

Figure 12. Offering forgiveness is like giving the offender a gift

Act out these three ways their conversation could go:

1. Sally tells Debbie, "I need to tell you honestly that I was hurt when you accepted the promotion that was based on work that I did, but after praying a lot, I do forgive you and I want us to have a good working relationship." Debbie says, "I didn't do anything wrong! If the boss offered you a promotion, wouldn't you take it? There's nothing to forgive me for!"

2. Sally tells Debbie, "I know what happened and why you got the promotion. I've had to pray about this for some weeks, but finally I forgive you for what you did." Debbie says, "OK, well it's no big deal. Some day you will get promoted, too. All in God's time."

3. Sally tells Debbie, "I know what happened and why you got the promotion. I've had to pray about this for some weeks, but finally I forgive you for what you did." Debbie says, "I have felt bad about this since it happened. At the moment, I couldn't think fast enough. You don't know this yet, but yesterday I went to the boss, and told him that you were the one who did all the work. He said he would be seeing you tomorrow to give you the promotion instead of me. I'm so sorry I did such a bad thing. Thank you for your forgiveness."

SMALL GROUP DISCUSSION

Share a time when you have offered forgiveness to someone. What happened? Was your experience more like Skit 1, 2, or 3, or was it completely different?

Give each small group a paper with one of the steps below written in big letters. Ask them to read the section, discuss it, and say it in their own words. Have representatives from each small group prepare to present their thoughts to the large group.

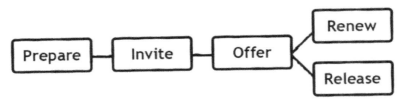

Figure 13. The process of offering forgiveness

Preparing for the meeting:

Prepare. Prepare your heart (See *Healing the Wounds of Trauma* lessons on Taking your Pain to the Cross and Forgiveness). Ask God for discernment and humility. Remind yourself that, as a human being, you could have committed the same offense. You may want to rehearse what you will say with someone you trust.

Invite. Get the right people, time, and place. This may involve just you and the other person, or it may involve others who are affected by the problem. In some cultures, this is done directly (*Matthew 18:18–17*) while others use a mediator. After inviting people, wait for them to respond.

At the meeting:

Offer forgiveness. Tell your story, including what happened and how you feel. Name the pain it has caused you. Tell them that they hurt you, and you forgive them and are not holding what they have done against them. Listen to their perspective and apologize for any real part you had in the problem. Ask them for what you need from them: for example, an explanation of why they did it, or that they listen to your story, or that they are sorry for what they did, or to make amends, or that you do not wish to see them again.

Renew or release. They may accept your gift or reject it—there are no guarantees. If the person admits their offense and accepts the gift of forgiveness, begin the work of rebuilding the relationship. This will take time, and they may need time to make amends. If you learned that you hurt them too, you may need to make amends as well. Do something to symbolize your mended relationship: for example, have a meal together, plant a tree, do a ritual, or say a prayer together. After much prayer and effort, if the person refuses your gift or if you risk being hurt again by the person, you may need to release the relationship, knowing you have made every effort to live with that person in peace. You do not wish them ill, but you no longer want them to be a part of your life.

Have the representatives from each group line up in order and share their feedback in the large group.

What is a good apology? (10 min)

1. Sometimes we are the ones who have caused an offense. Making a good apology and asking for forgiveness is difficult, especially if the offense was intentional.

Why can it feel difficult to apologize?

What is a bad apology?
What is a good apology?

Share feedback in the large group and then add anything from below that has not already been mentioned:
A bad apology:

> *I'm sorry, but ... (It was not my fault!)*
>
> *I'm sorry you feel that way. (You are the problem.)*
>
> *I'm sorry. I didn't mean to hurt you. (I'm innocent, really.)*
>
> *I'm sorry. I did the best I could. (I am good.)*
>
> *I'm sorry if I hurt you. (I don't think I did, but you think so!)*
>
> *I'm sorry, so forgive me—now!*
>
> *Saying I'm sorry over and over, even for things I was not responsible for. (I'm in such distress that you need to take care of me!)*
>
> *Saying I'm sorry but doing nothing to make amends.*

A good apology:

> *I take responsibility for hurting you.*
>
> *I listen to your story and feel your pain.*
>
> *I feel remorse and try hard not to do it again.*
>
> *I put my words of apology into action. I do what I can to make amends.*
>
> *I ask you to forgive me for what I have done.*

Like with offering forgiveness, if it is not possible or safe to contact the person, write your apology in a letter or tell it to someone standing in the place of the person you offended. This can help to relieve feelings of remorse.

---

5. How can I offer an apology and ask for forgiveness? (18 min)

The process for asking for forgiveness is similar to offering forgiveness.

Like in the exercise of offering forgiveness, give each small group a paper with one of the steps below written in big letters. Ask each group to read their section, discuss the content and notice how it is different than offering forgiveness. Have representatives from each small group prepare to present their thoughts to the large group.

Figure 14. Offering an apology and asking for forgiveness

Prepare and invite. Ask God for discernment and humility. The apology needs to come from your heart. It may be a private or public apology. Everyone who was affected by the offense needs to also be aware of your apology.

Admit the wrong you have done. Name the harm you have done and the way it has affected others. Tell the truth, even if it is shameful. Take responsibility for your actions. Answer any questions others may have honestly and thoroughly.

Witness their pain and apologize. Let them tell their story and listen without correcting details, arguing, or being defensive. After hearing their story, you may realize that you have hurt them much more than you realized and need to add to the list of hurts you have caused. Apologizing restores their dignity. If later they need to talk about it more, be willing to listen more.

Ask for forgiveness. "Will you forgive me?" Offer to make amends and commit to change your behavior. Don't try to force the offended person to forgive you on the spot. They may need time.

Renew or release (same as when offering forgiveness). If the person agrees to forgive you, accept this without trying to judge whether the person was sincere. Work to renew the relationship through having good experiences together. If the person does not accept your apology or does not wish to be in relationship with you, you can release the relationship, knowing you did your part.

Have the representatives from each group line up in order and share their feedback in the large group.

---

6. Closing exercise (7 min)

INDIVIDUAL REFLECTION

Prayerfully ask God to show you if you need to offer forgiveness to someone, or if you need to apologize to someone. Look at the steps of the processes above and sketch out a plan of action.

Pray for God's help.

Lesson 8. Fulfilling your purpose in life

Before you begin:

- For section 5: Provide large pieces of paper for each person at the tables. Have markers or colors available at each table.

In this lesson we will:

- Explore the importance of finding God's purpose for our lives.
- Discover ways to fulfill our purpose, perhaps turning our suffering into good.
- Discuss ways to take care of ourselves so that we don't burn out.

Lesson introduction

Trauma takes away our voice: we have no say in what happens. Work helps to restore our voice. It allows us to see that we have a role to play in the world, that we can influence our environment. Sometimes our purpose comes out of the trauma we have experienced.

To thrive, we need to fulfill the purpose God has for us. This may be in Christian ministry, education, science, arts, social work, politics, or any part of life. As we fulfill our purpose, we need to remember to care for our own needs so that we do not burn out.

1. Charles's story (10 min)

There was a young man named Charles who lived in Ibobo village. He was 22 years old and was finding it very hard to make money. One night when he knew a family was away for a few days, he crept into their house through a back window. He took their TV and filled an empty suitcase with their clothes. He crept out again and went home with what he had stolen. He started planning how to sell it.

He didn't know that a neighbor had seen him going into the house and carry things out. Early the next morning, the neighbor reported it to the police and the police went straight to Charles's house. They found him there with the stolen goods. They arrested him and he was given a sentence of two years in prison.

While in the prison, Charles attended trauma healing sessions and dealt with the shame he was feeling. He also gave his life to Jesus and asked Jesus to heal him. Charles discovered that he enjoyed working with wood in the prison carpentry class. At the end of his sentence he was released, and an NGO gave him a kit of carpentry tools.

He returned to the village and started making a living by making chairs and mending doors and windows of houses. He started attending church, and also joined a group of men who met once a week to pray for each other. An older man in the group gave him a lot of help. He started to feel happy and realized he was doing something useful that he enjoyed. He helped some widows mend their broken-down houses without asking for pay, and also started paying the school fees of a younger brother.

When he first got out of prison, he had felt ashamed because everyone knew he had been in prison, but as time went on, he was looked upon as a useful member of his community.

SMALL GROUP DISCUSSION

1. Why was it important that Charles found work he enjoyed?
2. After his return, how did he contribute to the community?
3. How did the church help?

Share feedback in the large group.

2. How can we find our purpose in life? (20 min)

Finding our purpose in life requires reflection and paying attention to how we feel as we engage in activities.

INDIVIDUAL REFLECTION

1. Think about what you do each day. Does it make you feel like a wilted plant or a plant that is flourishing? Explain.
2. What kinds of things make you flourish? What kinds of things makes you wilt?

Figure 15. Flourishing or wilting?

Share feedback in the large group.

Our purpose in life may be our job that provides an income, or it may be something we do in our free time, like a hobby, ministry, or volunteer work. We know we are fulfilling our purpose in life when what we are doing:

- challenges us and captures our imagination
- allows us to exercise our gifts and creativity
- allows us to feel pride in what we have done
- gives us joy, energy, satisfaction, and dignity

We can do any kind of work or ministry for a short time, but in the long run, we need to do things we find fulfilling or we will wilt like a plant without sunshine. This is not to say that a fulfilling life does not involve anything unpleasant! And our purpose may change over time.

Sometimes, our choices are limited, but there is always something, perhaps something small, we can do that brings us joy and satisfaction (*Jeremiah 31:2*). If we are in refugee camp, for example, we need to think creatively to find something we can do that brings us joy.

We are made in God's image. He worked to create the universe. We also work and are creative (*Genesis 1:28; 2:15, 19-20*). We can offer our work as a sacred act of worship to God (*Ephesians 6:5-7; Colossians 3:23–24*)

SMALL GROUP DISCUSSION

1. What do these verses teach us about living out our purpose in life?
2. How is work sacred?

   Exodus 31:1–5 (artists for tabernacle)
   Psalm 81:2 (musician)
   Genesis 4:21 (Jubal)
   Acts 9:36–39 (Dorcas)
   Acts 16:14 (Lydia)

Share feedback in the large group.

45

3. How can we live out our purpose? (15 min)

In all things, even when bad things happen to us, God works to bring good out of it, and we can help that process. Rather than being crushed by trauma, we may be able to get on top of it and use our pain for good. Our weakness may become our strength. For example, one man who was abused as a child started a ministry for vulnerable children which has helped hundreds of thousands of children around the world. In the Bible, Joseph's suffering led him to save his people and the Egyptians from starvation (*Genesis 50:20*).

Figure 16. Using your pain for good

SMALL GROUP DISCUSSION

Where do you find yourself in this illustration: being crushed by your trauma, or overcoming it and using it to bless others, or somewhere in the process?

Individual activity

Think about:

- Your skills, experience, and education
- Your community's needs: anything from practical needs to art or entertainment
- The resources available (not limited to funding)

Try to find ways these things come together. Filling out this sentence might help:

I could use my skill/experience/knowledge of _____ to help my community with their need for _____. To do this I would also need to get _____ (resources or help) from _____(who/where).

Share feedback in the large group.

Once you have identified something you could do that would help you experience more purpose in life, connect with others involved in this area, to learn from them and perhaps work together.

4. Putting boundaries around your work (20 min)

Your work can be so demanding or inspiring you need to put boundaries around it so you don't wear yourself out.

SMALL GROUP DISCUSSION

1. What do these Bible passages say about resting?

   Genesis 2:1–3

   Exodus 20:8–11

   Psalm 127:1-2

2. What does resting involve?
3. Is it different from sleeping?
4. What keeps you from resting?

Share feedback in the large group and then add anything from below that has not already been mentioned:

Resting shows that:

- we obey God's command to rest (*Genesis 2:2; Exodus 20:8-11*).
- we know everything does not depend on us. We are not indispensable. God's great love is at work in the world (*John 3:16*).
- we realize that even if we finish the work we have today, there will always be more!

Resting is different than sleeping. Rest involves:

- Making rest part of the rhythm of your life: every day, a day every week and, if possible, at least a week every year. For every mountain of activity, we need to plan to have a valley of rest.
- Finding something that is restful for us, that does not involve accomplishing a goal. It needs to be something unrelated to our normal work so we can come back to our work feeling refreshed. It may be playing sports, visiting friends, cooking, handiwork, or playing with children. For many people, it may require turning off cell phones and the internet.

Figure 17. For every mountain, there is a valley

- Identifying our sources of stress. It can come from:
  - trauma
  - people who want our help
  - good things that over-stimulate us.

The source of our stress does not matter to our bodies. Our bodies just feel that there is an emergency and they respond with an extra surge of strength and energy. We can become addicted to this energy surge and make it a way of life. If we do this, we will wear out our bodies and not be able to serve God or others. Rest is not optional.

DISCUSSION IN TWOS

1. What kinds of things do you find refreshing?
2. What challenges do you face to rest—each day, week, and year?
3. Why is it difficult for you to say "no" to others? To new opportunities?

Share feedback in the large group.

5. Closing activity (15 min)

Choose one of these activities:

1. *Make a drawing of you carrying out your purpose in life.*
2. *Make a drawing of the things you will do to take care of yourself. Place it where it will remind you of what you need to do.*

Lesson 9. Advocating for justice

Before you begin:

- For section 2: Prepare chart on flip chart paper.

In this lesson we will:

- Describe ways injustice works in a society.
- Identify groups in our communities who suffer from injustice.
- Discuss who should be involved in fighting injustice and what our part might be.

Lesson introduction

As we experience healing of our own trauma, we may feel drawn to help others who are suffering. These people may not be able to have difficult conversations because their voices are not heard. They need help both to recover from their suffering and to change the unjust structures that perpetuate their suffering. In this lesson, we look at speaking out against injustice. When we do, we not only reduce suffering, but we also fulfill our role as followers of Jesus in the world (*Luke 4:18-19*). People will see by our actions that God and Christians are concerned about justice.

1. Sam's story (15 min)

Sam lay in bed, unable to sleep. Through the wall, he could hear his neighbor boy being beaten brutally. This went on for some time. After a while, the boy's cries turned to weak whimpers.

Sam wrestled with his responsibility in this situation. He had heard the boy next door getting beaten before, but this time the father was in a rage and had lost control. Finally, Sam could take it no longer. He told his wife he had to do something about it. His wife told him it was not his business; it would be inappropriate to intervene. Sam tried to comply, but finally got up and called his friend, who was a policeman.

His friend arrived quickly. They went into the neighbor's home and got the boy out. Blood was everywhere. The father protested but could do nothing. The police took the boy to the hospital and then arranged for him to live with relatives.

Sam's neighbor never greeted him again.

After this incident, Sam and his wife worked with the police to help people in the neighborhood know that they should report cases of child abuse, and how to do it. By working together, child abuse was significantly reduced.

SMALL GROUP DISCUSSION

1. What risks did Sam take when he addressed the situation?
2. Who benefitted from the action Sam took? How did they benefit?
3. Who suffered from the action Sam took, and how did they suffer?
4. When is it appropriate to get involved helping people who are suffering injustice?
5. What did Sam and his wife do to address child abuse in their community?

Share feedback in the large group.

2. Understanding how power works (20 min)

God has given us power; he intends that we use it for the good of all. He has given each of us different gifts, abilities, and experiences (*Luke 19:11–27*). We each have different amounts of responsibility and power. Whatever amount of power we have been given, we should use to serve others, like Jesus did (*Matthew 20:25–28; Philippians 2:3–8*).

Injustice happens when people use their power to benefit their group and oppress others. Systemic injustice is when they create systems of laws, structures, and customs that oppress others.

An easy way to measure of the level of justice in a community is to look at the way it treats widows, orphans, and strangers (immigrants, refugees, displaced people).

SMALL GROUP DISCUSSION

1. How do people use their power to create unjust societies?
2. Who suffers in an unjust society? How do they suffer?
3. What things would you expect to see in a just society?

Share feedback in the large group and add anything from below not already mentioned:

When there is injustice:

   everyone suffers (*Proverbs 22:16; 1 Corinthians 12:26*), with some suffering more than others.

   there is no true peace.

It is in everyone's interest to work for justice.

LARGE GROUP DISCUSSION

Think of an issue of injustice in your community; for example, refugees, disabled people, trafficked people, women, or widows. Copy the left column of the chart on another paper that everyone can see.[10] Read the left column and think of how it applies to people with more power. Discuss how it applies to those with less power. Then read what is written in the right column of that row and discuss how that applies to your issue.

People with more power may:	People with less power may:
Protect the status quo, possibly using violence and political power to do so.	Be exposed to more violence and lack police protection. Be on alert all of the time for attack. Be afraid and intimidated.
Have many opportunities for income, education, housing, medical help, jobs, loans, etc.	Have few opportunities for income, education, housing, medical help, jobs, loans, etc.
Isolate themselves from the larger society and lose touch with the experience of others.	Be isolated and made invisible to the larger society; for example, mixed marriage may not be allowed, they may be forced to live in certain areas, etc.
Have the power to write history from their perspective.	Be ignored or misrepresented in the history of the area. Lose their identity.
Be blind to their privilege and not feel responsible for the way society works.	Lose hope: "Things will never get better. It's not worth trying."
Impose their culture on others.	Deny their identity to be accepted.
Be unaware that others are uncomfortable or face challenges.	Feel ashamed, that they are not good enough.
Feel they can express their emotions freely, including anger.	Need to contain their emotions, especially anger, around people with more power.
Be able to live comfortably.	Use all their energy to survive. Work hard to have bare essentials.

[10]Alternatively, if the group is small enough everyone can look at the page, just cover the right column.

INDIVIDUAL REFLECTION

How do you see yourself in these descriptions of people with more power and less power?

3. The Bible speaks about injustice (20 min)

God calls us to address injustice wherever we see it. All people are created in the image of God and need to be treated fairly and with respect.

SMALL GROUP DISCUSSION

Look up these passages and discuss how God feels about injustice:

Proverbs 17:15
Proverbs 6:16–19
Exodus 3:7-10
Psalms 89:14
Acts 10:34-35
Amos 5:14–15

Share feedback in the large group and then add anything from below that has not already been mentioned:

Justice is an important theme in the Bible. God hears the cries of the poor. He hates injustice (*Proverbs 6:16-19; 17:15*) and sends people to help (*Exodus 3:7–10; Psalm 89:14*). God welcomes and cares for all people without exception (*Acts 10:34–35*). He wants us to follow his example (Amos 5:14-15).

In *Isaiah 61:1–2*, we read how God heals people's broken hearts and comforts them in their grief. The passage goes on to compare them to trees that slowly grow and become strong and rebuild cities.

They will be like trees that the LORD himself has planted.

They will all do what is right, and God will be praised for what he has done.

They will rebuild cities that have long been in ruins. (*Isaiah 61:3–4*)

Serving those who are suffering is serving Christ (*Matthew 25:31–46*). This behavior pleases God (*Isaiah 58:6–12*).

SMALL GROUP DISCUSSION

How do you see the misuse of power in these passages?

Matthew 14:6-10
2 Samuel 11:1-17
Exodus 5:6-14

Share feedback in the large group.

4. Preparing to help (20 min)

Societies do not change quickly, and upsetting the status quo may be dangerous. People who are benefitting from the way things are may fight back. We need to prepare ourselves for a long effort with knowledge and patience (*Proverbs 19:2*).

First, we need to ask God to help us become aware of people suffering from injustice around us. This may be more difficult than we think! Our society may have:

- Removed people suffering from injustice from our view, either by killing them or keeping them out of sight.

- Made them act like us, giving up their dress, language, and culture, at least in public.
- Not considered them to be people the society is concerned about (*Luke 10:31-32*). They may be considered exotic and interesting, like scenery we take photos of, or we may think of them like machines who perform tasks for us. We may not see them as fully human and created in God's image. Injustice may be accepted as normal ("That's how life is here").

SMALL GROUP DISCUSSION

Who is suffering injustice in your community? Ask God to open your eyes to be able to see them.

SMALL GROUP DISCUSSION

Divide into groups according to church, ministry, or interests, and discuss these questions:

1. What structures, laws, and practices make life harder for this group? Do victims know their legal rights?
2. Who else is responding to this group--locally, nationally or globally?
3. Which of these groups that are responding can you work with? You cannot fight injustice alone.
4. What is your mission? Discuss what God might be calling you to do. You cannot do everything.

Share feedback in the large group.

5. Taking action (10 min)

SMALL GROUP DISCUSSION

1. What can you do to help advocate for justice?
2. How can you do it in ways that respect and empower people rather than make them feel like helpless victims?

Share feedback in the large group and then add anything from below that has not already been mentioned:

Awareness: Make a plan to speak out about the issue, to raise awareness, to make ways for the voiceless to be heard. Find ways to bring about change in the structures that perpetuate injustice: housing, education, medical services, voting, and so forth.

Accompany the vulnerable to get help: Connect them with existing resources.

Safety: Think through possible consequences of your actions for both advocates and victims.

Community: Help victims be a part of a community. For example, people released from prison may need a home and a job. They may need help learning how to function in society successfully. The church could be this community.

6. Closing exercise (5 min)

As you think about what you would like to do, what challenges do you anticipate?
Pray together for God's help and for those who are suffering from injustice.

Closing ceremony for equipping sessions

Make plans for how you can use these lessons with those who have already completed *Healing the Wounds of Trauma.* Share your plans with the group.
Then commission the facilitators using the suggestion below:

Presentation of the candidates to the officiating priest/pastor by the lead Facilitator

---

Lead facilitator: Servant of God, I present to you these people who have been trained in Bible-based Trauma Healing, that they may be commissioned for the service of Christ and his Church in the trauma healing ministry.

Priest/pastor: Have you taken care that these people you have presented to me for commissioning have been trained and fully qualified and are willing to serve Christ and his Church?

Lead facilitator: We have trained and examined them and found that they are worthy to be commissioned.

Priest/pastor: [*To Church Leaders and other people present*] Do you who are gathered here agree that these people be commissioned for the mission of Christ and his Church?

All: We agree.

Priest/pastor: [*To the candidates*] You who have been trained, examined and now presented to be commissioned for the service of Christ and his Church, I charge you in the presence of God and his Church and in the presence of this congregation that with your own lips and from your own heart you must declare your allegiance to Christ who called you to this ministry and to respond to these questions which I now put to you:

Priest/pastor: Will you be willing to lead trauma healing sessions in the Church of Christ wherever you may be called upon by the Church and her leadership?

Candidates: We will, God being our helper.

Priest/pastor: Will you pray for and support the body of Christ including the lonely, widows, and orphans and the weak and all others who need to experience the love of God while in difficult situations through the ministry of trauma healing?

Candidates: We will pray and support them, God being our helper.

Priest/pastor: Will you endeavor to be good stewards of God's creation and care for the people you are sent to?

Candidates: We will endeavor to do so.

Priest/pastor: Heavenly Father, we pray for these your servants whom we now commission to serve as trauma healing facilitators in the Church of Christ. May your Fatherly hand always be upon them that their ministry may meet the needs of your people who have experienced difficult situations and that they may receive your healing to the glory of your name. May your Holy Spirit be their guide at all times and lead them in the knowledge and obedience to your call upon their lives and that they may find fulfillment in this work and in their own lives through Christ, who lives and reigns with you forever and ever. Amen.

The Lord bless and watch over each one of you, that you may remain faithful servants as promised, and may the blessing of God Almighty, the Father, the Son, and the Holy Spirit be with you now and always. *Amen.*

Distribution of certificates
Closing prayer and benediction

Resources

1. Wrestling with God

Gutierrez, Gustavo. On Job: God-Talk and the Suffering of the Innocent. Maryknoll, NY: Orbis, 1987.

Katangole, Emmanuel. Born from Lament: The Theology and Politics of Hope in Africa. Grand Rapids, MI: Erdmanns, 2017.

O'Connor, Kathleen. Jeremiah: Pain and Promise. Minneapolis, MN: Fortress Press, 2011.

Africa Study application and proverbs and stories notes to the book of Job. Oasis International Limited, 2016.

2. Good and evil

Plantinga, Cornelius. Not the Way It's Supposed to Be: A Breviary of Sin. Grand Rapids, MI: Eerdmans, 1996. pp 158-162

McCord Adams, Marilyn. Horrendous Evils and the Goodness of God. Ithaca, NY: Cornell University Press, 2000.

Volf, Miroslav. Free of Charge: Giving and Forgiving in a Culture Stripped of Grace. Grand Rapids, MI: Zondervan, 2005.pp 95-96

Lewis, C.S. Mere Christianity. New York, NY: Harper One, 2001, pp 42-46.

3. Generational trauma and blessing

Healing the Wounds of Generational Trauma: The Black and White American Experience. Philadelphia, PA: American Bible Society, 2021.

Jennings, Willie James. The Christian Imagination: Theology and the Origins of Race. New Haven, CT: Yale University Press, 2010.

Laurence J. Kirmayer, Gregory M. Brass, Tara Holton, Ken Paul, Cori Simpson, and Caroline Tait. Suicide among Aboriginal People in Canada. Ottawa, Ontario: Aboriginal Healing Foundation, 2007. www.ahf.ca.

4. Shame and guilt

Thompson, Curt. The Soul of Shame: Retelling the Stories We Believe About Ourselves. Chicago, IL: IVP, 2015.

———. Anatomy of the Soul: Surprising Connections between Neuroscience and Spiritual Practices That Can Transform Your Life and Relationships. Chicago, Il: Tyndale, 2010.

Langberg, Diane. Suffering and the Heart of God: How Trauma Destroys and Christ Restores. Greensboro, NC: New Growth Press, 2015.

Langberg, Diane Mandt. Counseling Survivors of Sexual Abuse. Xulon Press, 2003.

Scazzero, Peter. The Emotionally Healthy Church: A Strategy for Discipleship That Actually Changes Lives, Updated and Expanded Edition. Grand Rapids, MI: Zondervan, 2010.

Flanders, Christopher L. About Face: Rethinking Face for 21st Century Mission. Eugene, OR: Pickwick, 2011.

de Silva, D.A. "Honor and Shame." In Dictionary of New Testament Background, edited by Craig A. Evans and Stanley E. Porter, 518–22. Downers Grove, IL: InterVarsity, 2000.

de Silva, D.A. Honor, Patronage, Kinship & Purity: Unlocking New Testament Culture. Downer's Grove, IL: InterVarsity Press, 2000.

de Silva, D.A. The Letter to the Hebrews in Social-Scientific Perspective. Vol. 15. Cascade Companions. Eugene, OR: Wipf and Stock Publishers, 2012.

McCord Adams, Marilyn. Horrendous Evils and the Goodness of God. Ithaca, NY: Cornell University Press, 2000.

Lau, Te-Li. Defending Shame: Its Formative Power in Paul's Letters. Grand Rapids, MI: Baker Academic, 2020.

https://www.ted.com/talks/brene_brown_listening_to_shame?language=en

5. Using our feelings for good

Lerner, Harriet. Why Won't You Apologize: Healing Big Betrayals and Everyday Hurts. New York, NY: Touchstone, Simon and Schuster, 2017.

McCombs, Margi, James Covey, and Kalyn Lantz. Healing Teens' Wounds of Trauma; How the Church Can Help Facilitator Guide, Philadelphia, PA: American Bible Society, 2017, 37-44.

Elliot, Matthew. Faithful Feelings: Rethinking Emotion in the New Testament. InterVarsity UK/ Kregel, 2006.

Thompson, Curt. The Soul of Shame: Retelling the Stories We Believe About Ourselves. Chicago, IL: IVP, 2015.

———. Anatomy of the Soul: Surprising Connections between Neuroscience and Spiritual Practices That Can Transform Your Life and Relationships. Chicago, Il: Tyndale, 2010.

Activity: Feelings map of your 'house'/self https://www.youtube.com/watch?v=gm9CIJ74Oxw

Hart, Archibald. The Anxiety Cure: You Can Find Emotional Wholeness and Tranquility. Nashville, TN: Thomas Nelson, 2001.

Brain video: https://www.youtube.com/watch?v=gm9CIJ74Oxw

6. Difficult conversations

Healing the Wounds of Trauma Advanced Facilitator Handbook 2016 version on interpersonal conflict

Patterson, Kerry, Joseph Grenny, Ron McMillan, and Al Switzler. Crucial Conversations: Tools for Talking When Stakes Are High. 2nd ed. McGraw Hill, 2011.

Stone, Douglas, and Sheila Heen. Thanks for the Feedback: The Science and Art of Receiving Feedback Well. London, UK: Penguin, 2014.

7. Living at peace with others

Volf, Miroslav. Exclusion and Embrace. Nashville, TN: Abingdon Press, 1996.

———. Free of Charge: Giving and Forgiving in a Culture Stripped of Grace. Grand Rapids, MI: Zondervan, 2005.

———. The End of Memory: Remembering Rightly in a Violent World. Grand Rapids, MI: Eerdmans, 2006.

Lerner, Harriet. Why Won't You Apologize: Healing Big Betrayals and Everyday Hurts. New York, NY: Touchstone, Simon and Schuster, 2017.

Tutu, Desmond, and Mpho Tutu. The Book of Forgiveness. San Francisco, CA: Harper One, 2015.

Lazare, Aaron. On Apology. Oxford, UK: Oxford University Press, 2004.

8. Fulfilling your purpose in life

Sayers, Dorothy. "Why Work?" In A Christian Basis for the Post-War World. England: S.C.M. Press, 1942.

Thompson, Curt. The Soul of Shame: Retelling the Stories We Believe About Ourselves. Chicago, IL: IVP, 2015.

———. Anatomy of the Soul: Surprising Connections between Neuroscience and Spiritual Practices That Can Transform Your Life and Relationships. Chicago, Il: Tyndale, 2010.

Mollica, Richard. Mollica, Healing Invisible Wounds: Paths to Hope and Recovery in a Violent World. Nashville, TN: Vanderbilt University Place, 2008.

Scazzero, Peter. The Emotionally Healthy Church: A Strategy for Discipleship That Actually Changes Lives, Updated and Expanded Edition. Grand Rapids, MI: Zondervan, 2010.

Hart, Archibald. Adrenaline and Stress: The Exciting New Breakthrough That Helps You Overcome Stress Damage. Nashville, TN: Thomas Nelson, 1995.

Buchanan, Mark. The Rest of God: Restoring Your Soul by Restoring Sabbath. Nashville, TN: Thomas Nelson, 2007.

Barton, Ruth Haley. Invitation to Solitude and Silence: Experiencing God's Transforming Presence. IVP, 2010.

9. Advocating for justice

Haugan, Gary. The Locust Effect. Oxford, UK: Oxford University Press, 2014.

Stevenson, Bryan. Just Mercy (Movie Tie-In Edition): A Story of Justice and Redemption. Spiegel & Grau, 2014.

Schreiter, Robert. The Ministry of Reconciliation: Spirituality and Strategies. Maryknoll, NY: Orbis, 1998.

O'Connor, Kathleen. Lamentations and the Tears of the World. Maryknoll, NY: Orbis, 2002.

Acknowledgements

The vision for this set of lessons came from Katherine Barnhart. She was in contact with trauma healing groups in various locations around the world who had bonded and matured by working through Healing the Wounds of Trauma together. They wanted to continue meeting and going deeper in their healing work together. Katherine looked for something she found sufficient but found nothing. With funding from Grove Foundation given to the American Bible Society, the work on this project began.

In 2018, Harriet Hill put a rough outline of topics together, then a small group composed of Godfrey Loum, Uwingeneye Baraka Paulette, Charles Adu Twumasi, Margaret Hill, met with her in Nairobi to determine the lesson topics and develop them. Over the following year, Harriet Hill worked with that input and completed drafting the lessons. Several experienced trauma healing facilitators helped write and adapt the stories. Trauma Healing Advisory Council members Dr. Richard Winter, Dr. Richard Baggé, and Dr. Phil Monroe gave feedback from a psychological perspective, and Peter Edman and Jeff Jue from a biblical perspective.

In October 2019, a group of 30 Trauma Healing facilitators from around the world met in Philadelphia to experience the lessons. This group and several from the Trauma Healing Alliance agreed to test them in their countries and translate them into their languages where needed. By March 2020, the feedback from those pilot testers was received and integrated into a final draft.

The efforts, expertise, and hard work of many people have gone into the making of Strength from Weakness. Our thanks to those mentioned, by name or group, and to all those who were not mentioned. And most of all, our thanks for the counsel of the Bible, which helps us navigate trauma so that we can recover and even flourish.

About the Author

Dr. Harriet Hill served as a linguist and Bible translator with Wycliffe Bible Translators and SIL International from 1979-2010, living in West Africa for 18 years. From 2001-2020, she was involved in Bible-based Trauma Healing and served as the main editor of the materials. In 2003, she completed her PhD at Fuller Seminary. From 2010-2020, she worked with American Bible Society in Trauma Healing. She is the author of many books and articles in Bible translation, Scripture Engagement, and Trauma Healing, and is developing as an artist.

CPSIA information can be obtained
at www.ICGtesting.com
Printed in the USA
LVHW062227031021
699419LV00010B/90

9 781585 163311